Church Planting
among
Immigrants
in
US Urban Centers:

The "Where", "Why", And "How"
of Diaspora Missiology in Action

Enoch Wan & Anthony Casey

Institute of Diaspora Studies – U.S.A
Copyright © 2014 by IDS-USA @ Western Seminary

This book is the sixth in a series on Diaspora Studies.

Published by the Institute of Diaspora Studies – USA
Western Seminary
5511 SE Hawthorne Blvd., Portland, OR 97215, USA

CHURCH PLANTING AMONG IMMIGRANTS IN US URBAN CENTERS: THE "WHERE", "WHY", AND "HOW" OF DIASPORA MISSIOLOGY IN ACTION

Enoch Wan and Anthony Casey

ISBN: 978-1502969668

For more information on IDS-U.S.A at Western Seminary or Enoch Wan, please visit the following sites:

- www.westernseminary.edu/diaspora
- www.enochwan.com
- www.GlobalMissiology.org

CONTENTS

Chapter 4

CHALLENGES IN URBAN, ETHNIC CHURCH PLANTING

PART 3 – UNDERSTANDING AND
IDENTIFYING ETHNIC GROUPS IN THE CITY

Chapter 5

ASSIMILATION THEORY AND PATTERNS

Chapter 6

IDENTIFYING AND UNDERSTANDING ETHNIC GROUPS IN THE CITY

Chapter 7

KEY ISSUES FOR EFFECTIVE URBAN, ETHNIC MINISTRY

PART 4 – DIASPORA MISSIOLOGY IN ACTION

Chapter 8

Chapter 9

Chapter 10

Part 1

INTRODUCTION

CHAPTER 1

INTRODUCTION AND PURPOSE

Regarding the Great Commission, "It has always been God's plan for the Church to go to the world, [however,] this strategy is only half of God's equation for reaching people who don't have a personal relationship with Christ" (Phillips 1997: 29). The world truly is at our door here in the United States. Some estimate that there are over 350 unreached people groups present in some capacity in the U.S. The U.S. ranks as the number one immigrant receiving country in the world, drawing more than 20% of all immigrants internationally. The majority of these immigrants come to the cities where they dream of new economic opportunity and freedom to pursue the "American Dream." People are on the move and God is at work, as He moves the nations (Jer. 31:7-14). The world is at our doorstep. The question is, who are these people and how can we reach them with the gospel of Jesus Christ?

Background

The authors[1] have worked in the diaspora context for many years, both overseas and in the United States. We have experiences working with immigrants of all types – college students, business folks, refugees, and religious leaders. We have been part of house churches, mega churches, and multi-cultural churches. Effective ethnic ministries in the U.S. can be hard to find, but many churches and individuals are trying as best as they can. We make sushi with Japanese students in college and in exchange we share a meal of squirrel we had hunted – both quite the cultural experience! We spend a summer in Chicago overwhelmed by the diversity we encounter as we step off the El train at the end of the red line into an Indian-Pakistani community where little English is found – either spoken or written. We get lost in the San Francisco Chinatown. We have tried many approaches to reach internationals, some successful, but many not. But we have learned much along the way.

---

[1] This book is a collaborative effort between the authors. We endeavor to write as one voice, therefore, do not distinguish who is writing when relating personal stories and examples. First person **"I"** is used primarily for the sake of conveying a more **personal tone** in the book. And at times, **"you"** is being used for a **conversation style.**

1

Purpose

Both of us have Ph.D. in anthropology/ missions and we have both taught at the seminary level; but we do not want this book to be an academic work full of anthropological theory and jargon. Rather, we want to combine the best of our academic training with the struggles we have had working with immigrants and planting ethnic churches and write something that is practical and helpful. At the end of this book, we hope you feel equipped to walk out your door, look at your neighborhood, and say "I have the theology, tools, heart, and motivation to understand who is here and how I can begin to reach them."

There are many good books available on immigration in general, even from the Christian perspective.[2] These books often give the 15,000 foot perspective – a flyover of the general contours of immigration, where are people moving, who generally is coming? These more demographic approaches are helpful; but there are not many books that help the church planter on the ground.

"Ok, the census tells me this many people from Iran live in my zip code, but where are they, what are they like, and how can I reach them?"

This book is the answer to that question. Yes, we will present general statistics on immigration; but we endeavor to show how immigration impacts the cultural identity and worldview of these immigrants. Immigration *changes* people, but how? As missionary anthropologist Paul Hiebert in essence said, "too often, we try to plant country churches in the city and don't know why we fail" (Hiebert 1995). It is not enough to just import in an effective suburban church model and think it will work in an inner city within the ethnic context. Immigration is complex and there is no one size fits all strategy. There are general patterns, however, that are helpful to know when beginning a church planting effort. In this book, we show these patterns of assimilation and integration that are common among immigrant groups. We also show how you can use the tools of cultural understanding to navigate in the city, talk to people, build relationships, gain entrance into these communities, find leaders, and plant healthy churches. These tools are important because you can carry them with you to any city. In some regard, it is impossible to tell somebody how to do ethnic ministry. The only legitimate answer is, "It depends!" This book hopefully can help you know "what it depends on" and "how to work effectively" in such situation.

---

[2]See for example, J.D. Payne, *Strangers Next Door: Immigration, Migration and Mission.* Downers Grove, IL: InterVarsity Press, 2012.

Key Terms

It is helpful to define a few terms you will see throughout this book. Without a clear definition, people often talk past one another. This book deals with church planting among immigrants in urban centers, so what do these terms mean?

Urban is difficult to define and some may say, "you know it when you see it!" The U.S. government actually calls any town with a population over 2,500 people "urban." Urban is a relative term. One of us spent time researching ethnic relations in Iqaluit, Nunavut, Canada near the Arctic Circle. Iqaluit is the capital and largest "city" in Nunavut with a burgeoning population of 6,000. Yet, when you consider the average village in Nunavut is only around 150 people, a town with a population 40 times larger than what you are used to seems massive! "What do you mean I can't shoot that caribou out of my bathroom window?" "Sir, you're in the city now…!" One of us lived in Louisville, Kentucky, a city with a metro population of close to 1 million. For many rural Southerners coming for seminary, the city was huge. Yet for students moving from Chicago or New York City, Louisville seems like a quaint small Midwestern town. Again, the urban experience is somewhat relative.

More descriptively, urban centers can be marked by density, diversity, and complexity. Cites pack a lot of people into a relatively small area. There are apartment complexes in Buenos Aires, Argentina that have more residents than all but a handful of cities in Wisconsin. Cities put people in close proximity to one another and force them to figure out some way to get along. The diversity that is characteristic of many cities makes that interaction a challenge. One can walk down the street in New York City and hear dozens of languages spoken. In fact, more than 800 languages are found in NYC! One intersection can have a church on one corner, a mosque on the other, and a Buddhist temple on the third. Cities assault people with sounds, smells, and sights that challenge our understanding of what is normal and acceptable.

Finally, cities are complex societies. There are many layers and networks of ethnicity, social class, and industry. This complexity poses a great challenge for church planters, as people relate to each other differently than they would in a mono-cultural small town where everyone knows everyone else. For practical purposes, when we write of cities in this book, we most often refer to those called Metropolitan Statistical Areas, which by definition have more than 50,000 people.

Urbanization is the process of city formation and growth, but more importantly, it explores how the city impacts its residents (Eames and Goode 1977: 30-70). People cannot live however they choose in a city; they are governed by laws, housing codes, zoning regulations, income, and a host of other factors that shape in many ways how people can form and express their cultural identity in an immigrant, urban environment. Urbanization then refers to how the city pressures and impacts the cultural production and identity of its residents.

Diaspora is a term that carries a plethora of connotations. Broadly, "diaspora" is simply a reference to people who have moved from their homeland and take up residence elsewhere, either internally or internationally. "Diaspora" differs from migration, however, in that diaspora peoples share a certain collective cultural consciousness, group identity, memory of the homeland, and some kind of social solidarity in the host country (Wan 2011). Diaspora peoples bring with them some level of their original cultural identity and seek to maintain that identity in the new setting.

Missiology is simply the system study of Christian missions. Typically, missiology includes a four-fold emphasis on theology, church history, understanding cultural understanding and ministry strategy. *Diaspora Missiology*, then, is the study of people away from homeland with an aim to understand and participate in God's redemptive mission among diaspora groups (Wan 2011).

Assimilation is the decline of an ethnic distinction and its corollary cultural and social differences. Ethnicity is a social boundary that shapes attitudes and actions toward others and helps groups form the boundary that allows them to say "they are not like us." Assimilation is not an one way endeavor, however, as change takes place on both sides of the ethnic boundary (Alba and Nee 2003). As assimilation occurs, an individual's ethnic origin becomes less relevant as individuals on both sides begin to see themselves as more alike than different. This definition of assimilation not only allows for the influence of the mainstream culture on immigrant groups; but also allows for movement by the mainstream toward cultural values of the immigrant group. Ethnic distinctions do not have to disappear; yet assimilation and integration is still possible.

Refugees are those individuals who, due to a well-founded fear of persecution due to race, religion, nationality, or political opinion, have left their home country and are now unable or unwilling to return. For example, there are many ethnic Nepali refugees now coming to the U.S. after they were forced out of Bhutan during a war two decades ago. They have spent the past years in refugee camps in Nepal, but the Nepalese government is unwilling to grant them citizenship. They are truly people without a home.

Urban Tribe is a heterogeneous group of people who share a common affinity that is stronger than their ethnic identity. This binding affinity may be shared status as refugees, college students, ESL learners, etc. In Nigeria, Housa and Yoruba peoples do not typically get along; but co-exit peacefully in a city in the U.S., due to the lowering of their ethnic identities and simply relate as "Nigerians" in an attempt to survive in an immigrant context. In essence, they move up a level with regard to the traditional understanding of a people group.

Orality is a complicated term that usually carries two distinctions: 1) Someone who cannot read or write or 2) Someone whose most effective communication and learning format, style, or method is not based on a literate approach. Oral peoples fall on a spectrum from primary oral learners with no exposure to the written word to highly literate peoples who always prefer their information in written form. However, true orality is about more than just a communication method or ability to read and write. Primary orality goes to the worldview level because it actually shapes to some degree how people view reality. Missiologist David Sills believes that oral peoples often view "truth" as relationship plus experience. In order for new information to be trusted and accepted, the hearer must have a relationship with the messenger and have some way to experience or apply the new information to their everyday life. Writing, in essence, removes the message from the messenger and breaks the relationship chain. Individuals of oral cultures often learn best through group oriented communication channels like story telling, singing, and ritualistic expression.

Chronological Bible Storying (CBS) is the sequential selection and telling of key stories from the Bible in a way that is faithful to the text; yet relatively easy for understanding, remembering, and reproducing by the hearer. CBS often presents the Bible in a Creation to Christ format, laying a biblical foundation for worldview change and helping the gospel message to make sense in light of the biblical understanding of God, man, sin, and salvation. A *storyset* is simply a collection of Bible stories that cover whatever topic is to be taught. For example, a storyset may contain ten stories focusing on what the Bible says about shame.

Regarding *church*, we include essential components like intentionality, identifiable membership composed of born-again believers, and movement toward regular worship, giving, evangelism, and local biblical leadership consisting of pastors and deacons. We realize that the church has many cultural expressions and denominational distinctive that are important; but not at the level to disqualify the entity from being a church.

Church Planting then is the intentional starting of new churches, primarily by means of evangelizing non-believers, and incorporating them into a local fellowship. We do not consider multi-site campuses to be separate churches, nor multiple services held at the same facility to be separate churches. We do consider a new church to have been planted, even if it meets in the same building as an existing church, if the new church is governed autonomously from the other congregations using the same facility.

Organization of the Book

You are reading Part 1 of this book now, which provides an introduction to the book and outlines its purpose, organization, and use.

Part 2 provides an orientation for church planting among immigrants in U.S. urban centers. Chapter 2 introduces the integrative approach to ministry we follow in this book, as well as laying out the biblical and theological foundations for ethnic church planting. Chapter 3 surveys recent immigration trends in the United States. Chapter 4 introduces challenges in urban, ethnic church planting including a discussion of the oral worldview.

Part 3 explores understanding and identifying ethnic groups in the city. Chapter 5 describes assimilation theory and the patterns of assimilation that are common among various ethnic groups in the United States. Chapter 6 covers tools for learning about people in your community, including a useful explanation of doing ethnographic research and using the information to contextualize ministry for that specific context. Chapter 7 discusses key issues in urban, ethnic ministry such as mono or multi-ethnic church planting, Chronological Bible Storying and other orality strategies, contextualization guidelines, mobilizing and training churches, and raising up indigenous leadership.

Part 4 draws the book together and discusses diaspora missiology in action. We discuss in Chapter 8 what diaspora missiology is, including the strategic nature of ministering in the diaspora context. Chapter 9 presents a suggested strategy for reaching ethnic peoples in each of the three assimilation models discusses earlier in the book, including answering five questions for each model: 1) How to access the people, 2) What language to minister in, 3) Appropriate orality strategies, 4) Addressing specific felt needs, and 5) What model of church is most likely effective? Chapter 10 concludes the main content of the book.

The two appendixes are designed to be copied and printed to use as workbooks to take into the community when conducting research. Appendix 1 is a worldview survey that asks helpful questions under the categories of Family, Friends, Food, Festivals, and the Future. Appendix 2 is an orality preference survey tool that can be used to identify where people are on the orality-literacy spectrum discussed in Chapter 4 and inform evangelism, preaching, and teaching strategies that are most appropriate for the context.

Practical Use

In general, this book is intended for established pastors and prospective church planters who desire to reach ethnic groups in their cities. We cover enough anthropological theory to lay a foundation to understand important dynamics of immigrant peoples, but provide practical how-to strategies for reaching people in your neighborhood. The appendixes are designed to be taken into the streets and used as research workbooks. We include many personal examples and stories of our attempts at ethnic ministry to illustrate our points, but also to show that this work is difficult at times, often uncertain, occasionally humorous; but always fulfilling.

We are free to try, fail, and learn because we find our identity in the God who never fails. The gospel reminds us that we are always accepted by our gracious God, not because of our merit or achievement, but because of Jesus who took our place on the cross and died the death we deserve. The gospel overcomes death and we are empowered by the same Spirit that raised Christ from the dead. Based on this truth, we can step out in faith with confidence that, as the apostle Paul understood, we must work while it is still daylight because God has many of his people our cities, just like in Corinth when Apostle Paul faced fierce resistance and hardship, Acts 18:9-10.

Part 2

ORIENTATION FOR CHURCH PLANTING AMONG IMMIGRANTS IN U.S. URBAN CENTERS

CHAPTER 2

MINISTERING AMONG IMMIGRANTS IN U.S. URBAN CENTERS: AN INTEGRATIVE APPROACH

Introduction

No expert of a single discipline and with myopic perspective can of help to those who desire to understand the complexity of urban context and to acquire comprehensive knowledge of immigrants from many lands. This chapter is an attempt to address this matter by proposing an integrative approach.

What is "an Integrative Approach" for Ministering among Immigrants in U.S. Urban Centers?

An "integrative approach" for ministering among immigrants in U.S. urban centers is "high-level synthesis of knowledge and skills of multiple disciplines and effective cooperation of related organizations for the sake of: gaining thorough understand of the complexity of urban context, acquiring comprehensive knowledge of diverse immigrants from many lands, and striving for cooperation/collaboration of related organizations to outreach and teach immigrants in U.S. urban centers for church planting."

There are three levels of integration (i.e. cognitive, practical and institutional) in the definition above, i.e. knowledge about urban context and diverse immigrants, skills in service/ministry to them and institutional cooperation for them, leading to church planting. We shall deal with each of these three aspects in further details after the brief explanation of the disadvantages due to lack of integration and the advantages of having integration.

11

Advantages and Disadvantages related to Integrative Approach

There are many disadvantages if an integrative approach is missing in the training of workers and in real life practice. For example, lack of integrative approach will lead to misunderstanding or fragmented knowledge of urban context that can cause conceptual confusion and ministry failure. Without integration, comprehensive knowledge of immigrants of many types (from student, refugee to professional) and from various backgrounds (e.g. geographic, religious and social aspects) is impossible.

Individually and institutionally, specialization is usually essential and helpful in knowledge and practice when serving in rural context and within homogeneous community. However, it is a total different ball game when it comes to navigating in urban context and serving diverse immigrants in U.S. urban centers. Without integration, nobody can address the complexity and face challenges posted by urban context and no single organization can have maximum effectiveness in evangelism, discipleship and church planting among diverse immigrants in U.S. urban centers. The consequences of lack of organizational cooperation and collaboration are service limitation, ministerial frustration, and operational futility.

Integrative approach is imperative due to the facts of situational complexity of urban context, ethnic diversity of immigrants and operational difficulty in outreach and challenge in edifying immigrants in U.S. urban centers for church planting. The advantages (why) and the ways and means (how) of integration at multiple levels in ministering among immigrants in U.S. urban canters for church planting are further elaborated in the next three sections in the order of preparation and practice as shown in the table below.

Table 1. Ministering among Immigrants in U.S. Urban Centers for Church Planting: An Integrative Approach

PROCESS	LEVEL	INTEGRATION	
PREPA-RATION	cognitive	knowledge	urban context
			diverse immigrant
PRACTICE towards church planting	practical	skill & methodology /ministry	missions *to* immigrant
			missions *through* the immigrant
			missions *by* & *beyond* the immigrant
	institutional	complementation /cooperation & partnership	missions *with* the immigrant

An integrative approach includes all three levels (i.e. cognitive, practical and institutional) and integration in terms of knowledge, skill, ministry method and organizational partnership are to be carried out through out the process.

Cognitive Integration: Understanding
Urban Context and Diverse Immigrants

In order to achieve cognitive integration in terms of preparation, there must be a basic understanding of the urban context and thorough knowledge of diverse immigrants as shown in the table above.

An integrative approach can bridge social and behavioral sciences for a better understanding of the complexity and challenges of the urban context for church planting. An integrative approach will empower workers with both knowledge and skills gleaned from various disciplines, from biblical studies, cultural analysis, missiological understanding and ministerial implementation.

Disciplinary integration will enhance understanding of the phenomena of modernization, urbanization, and globalization related to city of the 20th century. There is disciplinary synergism for a comprehensive understanding of city and the residence therein. There is also a necessity of methodological integration in research, combining ethnographic, bibliographic, demographic data and field research. See Chapter 6 for details and publications by Enoch Wan.[3]

Immigrants are to be viewed holistically including physical, psychological, social and spiritual dimensions. They come from many lands, multiple geographic locations, different historical and religious contexts, and are of various social strata. Therefore, disciplinary integration in preparatory knowledge of immigrants in U.S. urban centers is imperative. Integration of knowledge about diverse immigrants from disciplines such as history, geography, anthropology, comparative religious studies, sociology, etc. are essential for a comprehensive understanding for pre-evangelism, evangelism, discipleship and church planting. For detailed discussion on this matter, see Chapters 3 and 4.

---

[3] Wan, Enoch. "Rethinking Missiological Research Methodology: Exploring a New Direction." *Global Missiology* (October 2003). Available at www.GlobalMissiology.org.

_____ "The Paradigm and Pressing Issues of Inter-disciplinary Research Methodology." *Global Missiology* (January 2005). Available at www.GlobalMissiology.org

Practical Integration: Skills/Expertise in Service/Ministry to Diverse Immigrants

After the necessary preparation (at the cognitive level), practical integration of knowledge with skills and organizational partnership will enable Christian workers to engage in missions *to, through, by/beyond* and *with* immigrants in urban centers in U.S. cities.

An integrative approach bridges social, behavioral sciences by understanding the linkage between multiple factors related to immigrants in urban context. It is vital that integration occur in all steps of the ministry process: in theory, research design, data collection, data analysis, ministry planning and implementation of strategy (Wan 2014, chapter 10). It is important to combine knowledge and skills into one unified system when serving immigrants in urban context in U.S. cities. For further details on these points, please refer to discussions in Chapter 5 and Chapter 6.

Institutional Integration: Cooperation for Evangelism Discipleship, and Church Planting

Churches and para-church organizations might each have diverse heritage, gift-set, and expertise in "missions *to*" and "missions *through*" the immigrants in service, evangelism, discipleship and church planting. Therefore, cooperation and partnership will be possible if all can share a Kingdom-orientation; instead of denominational demarcation, parochial attitude, partisan spirit and negative competitition. Evidence is required on the linkage between personal evangelism, discipleship and the training/development of workers for church planting. In terms of program planning and implementation[4], there can be high-level integration that is organizational and institutional by entering into partnership. Integration can occur in all steps of the ministry process by seeking complementation of expertise of different organizations of all types: ranging from housing, community service, ESL, evangelism, and discipleship. Complimentary effectiveness in operation is possible by forming a higher level (i.e. city-wide or regional new entity) to achieve organizational integration for ministry fruitfulness in outcomes. Detailed discussion can be found in Chapters 7 and readers are referred to the case studies (chapters 17, 18, 19) in *Diaspora Missiology: Theory, Methodology and Practice* (Wan 2014)

---

[4] Wan, Enoch and Kevin Penman. "The 'Why,' 'How' and 'Who' of Partnership in Christian Missions," *Global Missiology* April 2010. Available at www.GlobalMissiology.org

Summary

In this chapter, we begin with a description of the complexity of urban context in U.S. cities where most immigrants reside and the diversity of them in terms of background and style. Preparatory understanding of the complexity of urban context and diversity of immigrants is prerequisites before engaging in ministry among them. Knowledge and skills gleaned from various disciplines are to be integrated in ministry *to* immigrants, motivating and mobilizing them (*by and beyond*). Institutional integration in the formation of new but high-level organization (e.g. city-wide or regional entity), and organizational partnership will lead to synergistic effectiveness and fruitful outcomes.

CHAPTER 3

IMMIGRATION TRENDS AND PATTERNS IN THE UNITED STATES

Introduction

Global migration is happening at an astounding rate. In 2013, of the just over 7 billion people in the world, 232 million were living in a country they were not born in. Put together in one place, migrants would compose the fourth largest country in the world and they are becoming a force in global trends from economics to education.

The majority of these migrants (over 60%) now live in the most developed areas of the world – the cities. More than ever before, these migrants are of working age, between 20 and 60 years old and are sending money – remittances – back to their home countries in vast sums, over $500 billion a year. In some countries, money sent back by immigrants accounts for up to 8% of the country's entire Gross Domestic Product. Over 90% off all immigration occurs for economic reasons as people seek a better permanent life elsewhere, or just want to work a few years in London, Tokyo, or New York City, send money back, and then return and live comfortably for the rest of their lives.

In general, immigration is a wave that does not appear to be slowing down and has been increasing significantly over the last twenty years. Peoples on the move are changing the face of global life and present unique ministry opportunities all over the world as people are pushed, pulled and uprooted to new locations.

Trends in the United States

The United States is by far the largest receiving country of global immigrants. More than 20% of all immigrants settle in the U.S., while Russia is a distant second, receiving around 12% of global migration, mainly from former Russian speaking Soviet countries with names ending in "~stan." The world truly is at our door here in the U.S. The statistics are staggering. In 2013, nearly 46 million of the United States' 315 million people were born somewhere else. Over 1 million people were granted legal immigration status in 2012 alone.[5] Nearly 70,000 were given refugee or asylum status. The Mexico-U.S. corridor passes the largest number of immigrants of any in the world. As of 2013, there were more than 13 million Mexicans living in the U.S. Aside from those permanent residents, another 162 million were granted short-term, non-immigrant admission to the United States, as tourists, students, or business people. Overall, more than 165 million people entered the United States for one reason or another in 2012 from every nation on earth.

International Students

The U.S. is the largest destination for international students as well. The Institute for International Education reports that more than 800,000 internationals studied in the U.S. in 2013. The top four countries sending students were China, India, South Korea, and Saudi Arabia, with the most growth occurring with Chinese and Saudi students. Three of these four countries contain some of the largest numbers of unreached peoples in the world, as well as the lowest percentage of Christians.

Competition to study in the U.S. is so high that a recent BBC report indicated that in China, up to 90% of students cheat in some way on their exams to be among the top students and most likely to be considered for study overseas. A Singaporean friend told me that the top university in Singapore is regularly the second choice for the country's top students – any university in the United States takes priority and students do all they can to earn admission to a U.S. school.

Refugees and Asylum Seekers

The U.S. is also receives a large number of refugees and asylum seekers each year. In 2012, more than 70,000 entered the United States. The top five sending countries were: Bhutan – 15,000, Burma – 14,000, Iraq – 12,000, Somalia – 5,000, Sudan – 1,000.

These countries contain huge numbers of unreached peoples as well and we have a great, God-given opportunity to receive, love, and minister to these refugees here in the United States. Boston, Dallas, and Louisville are key cities

---

[2]The statistics for U.S. immigration were compiled primarily from the United States Department of Homeland Security, Yearbook of Immigration Statistics: 2012. This pdf document is available at http://www.dhs.gov/publication/yearbook-2012

that receive large numbers of refugees and already have government programs and ministries in place to work with the specific needs of refugees.

Trends in Urbanization

Urbanization describes city-based processes related to city formation and growth. Urbanization also addresses the way social networks use urban space and how micro-societies relate to one another within the broader complex urban population. Urban areas are constantly changing, whether growing in population and infrastructure like Las Vegas or declining like Detroit. The overarching trend, however, is that the United States has been urbanizing at a rapid pace. The U.S. urban population increased by 12.1% from 2000 to 2010, outpacing the nation's overall growth rate of 9.7% for the same period, according to the U.S. Census Bureau.[6] Many cities grew at a tremendous pace during the ten year period, none more than Palm Coast, Florida which grew by 92% between the last two census readings.[7] Growth of the ten largest cities in the United States accounted for nearly a quarter of the total population growth in the United States from 2000 to 2010.

The proportion of new urban dwellers that are also immigrants is likely to be high. More than half of all foreign born peoples living in the United States live in one of four states: California, New York, Texas, and Florida. Among the 40 million foreign-born residents in 2010, 82.6% reported a year of entry prior to 2005. The remaining 17.4 percent entered from 2005 to 2010.[8] These figures reveal a large percentage of first generation immigrants living in the United States and are the primary subject of this book. How are these immigrants integrating to life in the U.S.? Are they learning English? Do they retain their worldview, religious affiliation, and cultural identity or are they assimilating and taking on characteristics of American culture?

Foreign Born in North American Cities

Church planters should consider cities in Canada as well. Canada is seeing increased immigration and urbanization particularly among immigrants. Payne notes that many migrants to Canada "are predominantly urbanites and are even more likely to live in a metropolitan area than Canadian-born citizens. In 2006, 94.9 percent of the foreign-born population

---

[3] U.S. Bureau of the Census, "Growth in Urban Population Outpaces Rest of Nation," http://www.census.gov/newsroom/releases/archives/2010_census/cb12-50.html.
[4] U.S. Bureau of the Census, "Population Distribution and Change: 2000-2010," http://www.census.gov/prod/cen2010/briefs/c2010br-01.pdf, 4.
[5] Nathan P. Walters and Edward N. Trevelyan, "The Newly Arrived Foreign-Born Population of the United States: 2010," under "American Community Survey Briefs," U.S. Department of Commerce Economics and Statistics Administration, 1, http://www.census.gov /prod/ 2011pubs/acsbr10-16.pdf.

and 97.2 percent of the recent immigrants lived in either a census metropolitan area or a census agglomeration [i.e., urban community]" (Payne 2012: 43). Major cities in Canada such as Hamilton, Winnipeg, Calgary, Vancouver, and Toronto have foreign born populations comprising 25% to nearly 50% of the city's population, and this growth is not slowing down.

The following chart shows the U.S. cities with the largest foreign born populations. Church planters can use this information to determine which cities to target by sheer numbers alone.

Table 1. Top 20 U.S. Cities with largest foreign born populations

City	Net Immigration
New York	128042
Miami	52706
Los Angeles	49798
Washington	36871
Houston	25504
Boston	24116
Chicago	23646
San Fransisco	23534
Dallas	19501
Philadelphia	17520
Seattle	17044
Atlanta	16910
Orlando	14725
San Jose	14124
San Diego	11720
Minneapolis	10374
Detroit	10366
Tampa	9769
Phoenix	8437
Baltimore	8287

While this type of demographic research is motivating and helpful, it does have its limitations. The census can only determine the country of origin of immigrants and cannot list which people groups are represented in these cities.[9] That research is much more difficult to determine and is largely the focus on the rest of this book.

---

[9] One ministry, Global Gates, in New York City is producing outstanding people groups research in the city. See their website at www.globalgates.info.

J.D. Payne, in his recent e-book *Unreached Peoples, Least Reached Places*[10], lists the following information compiled from a variety of sources on specific people groups scattered around U.S. cities:

- El Cajon, California is home to "Little Bagdad," with 60,000 **Iraqis**
- Of the 30,000 **Senegalese** in New York, over half are **Wolof Mourides**
- The Bay Area of California is home to "Little Kabul," and made up of tens-of-thousands of **Afghans**
- Minneapolis, Seattle, and Columbus, Ohio are home to well over 100,000 **Somalis**
- Irving, Texas is home to 5000 **Kurds** with Nashville housing the largest number in the country
- **Punjabi Sikhs** number 80,000 in New York
- St. Louis is home to the largest number of **Bosnians**, with estimates ranging between 35,000-60,000.
- Detroit has the largest concentration of **Arab Muslims** (e.g., **Yemeni, Iraqi, Lebanese, Palestinians**) numbering in the tens-of-thousands.
- Outside of Israel, New York is home to the largest number of **Jews** in the world, numbering in the millions
- About 5000 **Soninke/Serecole Muslims** live in New York
- Second to metro New York with 60,000, South Patterson, New Jersey is home to thousands of **Egyptian Arab Muslims**
- 89,000 **Tamils** live in the United States, with the largest concentration in Central New Jersey
- **Albanians** (**Tosk** and **Gheg**) number 122,000, with the largest numbers living in New York, Chicago, Boston, and Detroit
- A few hundred thousand **Urdu** may be found in the United States with large concentrations in Houston, New York, Los Angeles, Chicago, Seattle, and Atlanta
- **Turks** are estimated at 378,000 with the largest enclave found in the South Patterson area of New Jersey
- The **Burmese** have significant populations in New York, Los Angeles, Bay Area of California, Dubuque, Iowa, and Fort Wayne, Indiana

[10]The free pdf book is available at http://www.jdpayne.org/2014/03/03/free-ebook-unreached-peoples-least-reached-places/. JD's book is an excellent accompaniment to this book.

Literacy Background of Immigrants

Many of these immigrants come from developing countries where literacy rates are low, but it is difficult to exclusively determine the level of oral culture preference immigrants bring with them. Current research on immigrants and literacy focuses on the process of learning to speak, read, and write English. For example, there are roughly 22,500,000 Limited English Proficiency (LEP) adults, accounting for 10% of the U.S. adult population and comprising 9% of the labor force.[11] The overwhelming majority of LEP adults are immigrants.

These statistics only account for immigrants' abilities in English and little research is available on the literacy capabilities of these immigrants in their mother tongue. However, an interview with an ESL teacher informed me that the majority of those learning English through agencies in Louisville, Kentucky cannot read or write well in their mother tongue. These agencies only focus on teaching immigrants English and rarely consider the cultural background of the student.[12] My own experience with immigrants resonates with Lindgren's thoughts.

Summary

The world is at our door, there is no question about that. Let this brief overview of immigration statistics and trends challenge you to consider the great need and the great opportunity of diaspora missions in the United States. God is the mover of nations, and there is no coincidence that these millions of peoples from unreached countries have come to the U.S. The questions are now, who are these people, where are they in our cities, and how do we reach them with the gospel?

Christian anthropologist Darrell Whiteman remarks that

> as urbanization and globalization come together in the megacities of the world, they present incredible opportunities but also tough challenges for the church. [However,] insights from urban anthropology can help us understand the tremendous rural to urban migration of people all over the world and why migrants are often more open to religious innovation when they move to the city. Anthropology can reveal how people move from rural kinship to urban social networks as the primary organizing principle of people in cities (Whiteman 2006: 66-67).

---

[11]Chandasi Pandya, "Limited English Proficient Workers and the Workforce Investment Act: Challenges and Opportunities," http://www.migrationinformation. org/Feature/display.cfm?ID=900 (accessed August 29, 2012).

[12]Dana Lindgren, interview by author, Louisville, KY, August 24, 2012. Lindgren teaches ESL for two organizations in Louisville and expressed a lack of training to handle the cultural traits immigrants bring with them. Of particular challenge are those immigrants coming from oral preference backgrounds who, consequently, are the majority of immigrants needing ESL services.

It is precisely the challenges of reaching these global migrants, understood through the framework of urban anthropological theory, that form the core of this book. The next two chapters address the specific challenges of urban, ethnic ministry and then describe general assimilation, integration, and settlement patterns of immigrants in cities. This research forms the basis for the church planting strategies recommended in Chapter 9.

CHAPTER 4

CHALLENGES IN URBAN, ETHNIC CHURCH PLANTING

Introduction

Churches are moving toward efforts to reach urban dwellers in the United States. The North American Mission Board (NAMB) of the Southern Baptist Convention is one of the larger church planting networks in North America. NAMB has recently moved toward an emphasis on urban church planting. This urban priority has surfaced especially after Aaron Coe became the agency's vice president for mobilization. Coe states that cities are "the mouthpiece of any nation and the place where culture is created."[13] NAMB believes that if it reaches the cities, it can reach the world and is launching efforts to plant churches in fifty key North American metropolitan areas. Other church planting networks such as Acts 29 and the Sojourn Church Network are also heavily focused on urban areas.

The evangelical church in North America has not been particularly focused on urban ministry the past several decades. The rise of the mega-church era beginning in the 1980s was mainly focused in wealthy suburbs. White flight and other mass exoduses of inner city residents in the mid-twentieth century began to fuel a suspicion of cities as dangerous and undesirable places. They were places to visit for shopping or entertainment, but if one had the means, the suburbs were the "ideal" places to live. Drives into the city often resulted in locked car doors and increased heart rates until "safe" arrival occurred. Thankfully, this unbiblical and unhealthy sentiment is changing and cities are once again increasingly seen as key places for life and ministry. Cities are places of high levels of immigration and diversity and pose

---

[13] North American Mission Board, "Why Send?," https://www.namb.net/overview-why-send (accessed May 15, 2012). I do not agree that cities are the only place culture is created and disseminated. Rural communities have their own traditions and cultural expressions that may not be related to surrounding metropolitan areas in any way. I include this quote from Coe simply to show that NAMB is placing a priority on city ministry, partially because they feel cities are the primary place for the creation of culture.

23

unique challenges for ministry. Church planting among immigrants is not the same as reaching people of our own culture. There are many unexpected challenges that we must be prepared to face. A good first step is learning from those who have gone before us to see what we can gain from their experiences.

Urban, Ethnic Church Planting in North America

Much has been written on church planting in general, but we still have much to learn to minister well in the urban, ethnic context. This section presents challenges to ethnic ministry and insights from those who have worked in urban context both in North America and internationally.

Learning from the North American Context

Historically, church planting books for the North American context have been broad and provide little insight into ethnic church planting in urban centers. Ed Stetzer, one of the most recognized authors and speakers on North American church planting notes that "although most growth in church planting in recent years has occurred among ethnic groups, comparatively little has been written on the subject" (Stetzer 2003: 159). Stetzer describes several ethnic church planting models, broken into two broad categories. He first describes models that fit the context of an anglo church desiring to plant a new ethnic church. First is the natural birth model where an existing, and likely anglo church, plants a new church in an ethnic community geographically distant from the home church. Second, a sponsoring church finds an existing ethnic church in another neighborhood and adopts it to help in its development. Third, the implantation model consists of a sponsoring church beginning an ethnic mission in its own building and then transplanting the church out into the neighborhood once it begins to grow.

Next, Stetzer provides models that work with churches who wish to use their building and allow more than one church to meet. Stetzer notes the multi-worship service where multiple ethnic groups worship simultaneously but in different parts of the church in order to accommodate linguistic needs. Next, some church may use one corporate worship service in one language but provide small groups or Sunday School divided linguistically and culturally. Finally, Stetzer notes the multicultural church where the church is integrated but designs services for a variety of cultural groups. There are other good books on general church planting such as J.D. Payne's *Discovering Church Planting* (Payne 2009), but these books do not provide a lot of insight into the specifics of the actual process of ethnic church planting. To that end, a survey of books on international church planting can be helpful.

Learning from the International Context

More recently, a new group of literature is circulating, most of which interacts with the idea of Church Planting Movements. Mission agencies like the International Mission Board of the Southern Baptist Convention began to use creative means to access peoples in countries that were closed to missionary presence starting in the 1980s. Strategies were developed to quickly and efficiently reach and train nationals so they were equipped to plant churches among their own people. As these "movements" began to take shape, men like David Garrison studied them and attempted to draw out general principles common to the rapid acceleration of church growth (Garrison 2004). Some churches and mission agencies in the U.S. are adopting these strategies to reach immigrants in our cities. One example is Global Gates, a ministry in New York City founded by two former missionaries.

Missions strategy in general has moved from western based models where missions efforts and local pastorates were occupied by foreigners or outsiders toward a model that Tom Steffen calls the facilitator era (Steffen 2011). The trend today is empowerment of nationals to carry out the remaining task of reaching the nations including church planting, Bible translation, leadership training, and even formal Bible school and seminary schooling. These authors and their works challenge the typical American church planting model where one person plants and then pastors one church for a number of years. U.S. church planters should consider more of a catalytic model where each church plant is viewed as a training center to send out additional church plants. The sheer numbers of ethnic peoples in U.S. cities means that a more creative approach is necessary and many books focused on international missions offer helpful insights into reaching ethnic peoples in the U.S.

Particularly helpful are authors of these books emphasize on the need to understand the challenging cultural dynamics of the immigrants. Paul Hiebert, perhaps the preeminent missionary anthropologist of the 20th century, draws a close connection to the value of cultural anthropology to the task of missions and church planting. Hiebert writes that in past generations, church planters understood the Scriptures well but did not understand the people they served (Hiebert 1994). The result of cultural misunderstanding is that message is not understood, churches look foreign to the context, and churches can never become self-supporting financially. Hiebert notes that all people live in a specific context: that of their family, neighborhood, city, and nation. Yet, most people do not give specific thought to these issues and how they shape the worldview and perception of what is true, right, and proper. People inevitably assume everyone is like them. Hiebert observes that oftentimes, "only when things go wrong, or change rapidly, or when our views of reality conflict with the assumptions from another culture do we question them" (Hiebert 2009: 17-18). In the midst of these crises, cultural anthropology can help the church planter make sense of why things are going wrong in the new cultural setting, or, how to avoid the problems in the first place.

Anthropology helps the church planter discover the worldview of the target people. Basically, worldview dictates how people perceive reality and provides the basis for what they value with regard to religious beliefs and social relationships – two key categories for church planting. Without an awareness of the distinctives of culture, ethnicity, and social grouping, a church planter may inevitably treat all people the same. Such an approach fails to take into account the diversity of God's creation and the expression the church can take in a variety of cultural contexts.

Learning from the Urban Context

Harvie Conn and Manuel Ortiz, at the full maturity of their thought on urban ministry, published a comprehensive guide to urban ministry (Conn and Ortiz 2001). Their *Urban Ministry* is more suited to the questions this book seeks to answer and identifies several key issues and challenges present in urban ministry in general.

The place (primacy) of the city. As noted above, urban anthropologists have begun to study the city itself and examine how law, codes, and urban planning and design work to create culture within the city. Conn and Ortiz seek to demonstrate how urban centers are at the center of culture production, a place where religion, politics, and sheer numbers of people come together and influence both the local and global culture. Additionally, McMahan lists ten key reasons why the city is strategic: Numbers of people, opportunity, freedom for people to explore their beliefs, receptive people, receiving centers for immigrants, world influence, cultural center, cities are on travel route cross-sections, cities can meet holistic needs of people, and cities are places for renewal and reinvention (McMahan 2012: 1-18). Essentially, cities are places of influence, power, and possibility regarding cultural production and missiological opportunity.

Research needs. The complexity and diversity of the city leads to difficulty in understanding the specific realities that individuals face in their own neighborhoods. The only way to learn of these realities is through research. Yet, J.D. Payne writes that historically, evangelicals have not placed much confidence in research (Payne 2012: 139). Thankfully, times are changing. The creation of worldwide evangelical research databases like the Joshua Project, IMB Global Research, and the World Christian Database showed the usefulness of people groups research for missions strategy.

These groups mainly focus overseas, however, and Payne feels that evangelicals in many ways have a better understanding of peoples across the oceans than we do in our own backyards here in the U.S. and Canada. He writes "we have little to no knowledge of the peoples in our neighborhoods"

(Payne 2012: 140). What Payne is referring to is the lack of ground level understanding of people groups in cities. Census data and demographics can only provide what Payne calls the "15,000 foot perspective." At this level, one can only find that there are pockets of Somalis living in a zip code. The census cannot tell where they precisely live, what specific people groups are there, whether they have an evangelical presence or not, and what their social relationships are with other people in the area through which the gospel could travel. Only street level anthropological research can answer these important questions. These authors and urban ministry practitioners see the value of research, both demographic and ethnographic in nature, to effectively minister in the city.

Diverse strategies for church planting. Research reveals the diversity of peoples and their social settings in urban environments. The outcome of these findings should lead to multiple strategies for church planting. Many authors identify strategies involving addressing felt needs of urban dwellers. Ellison notes that the clamor of urban life pulls peoples' attention in many different directions. Addressing felt needs (1) provides a point of redemptive contact – it builds a genuine relationship, (2) felt needs ministries add credibility to the communication of the gospel, and (3) the Scriptures command ministry in word and deed (Ellison 1997: 94-110). However, felt needs differ depending on the background of the immigrant. The standard approach of teaching ESL, driving lessons, and helping immigrants prepare for the U.S. citizenship examination is not applicable in every context. Baker points out the need for addressing reconciliation because the city brings together peoples who may have traditionally been at war or the subject of oppression and discrimination (Baker 2009: 109-76). Conn and Ortiz make a case for a holistic ministry and social transformation that extends beyond the individual to the community itself (Conn and Ortiz 2001: 340-57).

A further challenge is that urban centers contain a variety of population segments. There are some who insist on a multi-ethnic approach to church (DeYmaz 2007), though most works argue for a contextualized approach to reach various social and ethnic groups in the city. Harvie and Conn argue for appropriate strategies for populations of immigrants, with linguistic and cultural distinctions, and then other strategies for the poor in the city, with their social distinctions (Conn and Ortiz 2001: 311-39). The multi-ethnic church question is crucial for urban church planting and will be addressed further in Chapter 7.

Aspects of training leaders in urban contexts. A final challenge authors deem crucial for urban ministry is the selection and training of leaders in the urban context. Conn and Ortiz suggest there are three kinds of leaders in the urban context (Conn and Ortiz 2001: 379-86). The first is the relocated leader who moves to the city from a distinctly different context. The second is the indigenous leader who grew up in the city and belongs to a particular cultural group in the city. The third kind of leader is the multiethnic leader. This type of leader networks and partners with the diverse array of ethnic leaders found in center city contexts and has the aptitude to navigate interculturally. These authors warn against overlooking the indigenous leadership that may already be in place in the community in favor of bringing in a relocated leader who is unfamiliar with the context and does not have the trust of the local people. This is a needed warning, as many larger Anglo churches in the U.S. are used to hiring in "A-list" leadership if possible. Such an approach is neither feasible, nor healthy in ethnic church planting context.

Appropriate models of mentorship, along with formal and informal theological education are important in the urban context. People in the city have a variety of cultural and educational backgrounds that must be considered when developing training programs. Are the leaders from a highly oral culture where intensive hands-on learning is essential and literacy based, classroom style teaching is ineffective? How does the teacher build trust in a trustless urban environment? How does one motivate urban leaders to stay in the city and start new works? Mentoring and theological education of some kind is crucial for the longevity and health of ethnic churches (Sills 2010). The urban environment brings unique challenges for training leaders and one that must be taken seriously for effective ministry.

Orality Issues within Ethnic Ministry

One of the most formidable challenges in ethnic ministry is how to minister to immigrants who cannot read and write or have extremely low levels of literacy. Compounding the difficulty is the fact that so little has been written on orality. Many western, educated American church planters have little conception of the worldview and learning style of oral-preference peoples and, consequently, approach ministry to them the same way they would minister in their own literate congregations. For this reason, we provide a thorough explanation of the oral worldview in order to reorient church planters to the very different dynamics of oral cultures.

It has been written, "the gospel is being proclaimed now to more people than at any other time in history, yet many of those are not really *hearing* it" (Claydon 2005: 3). The problem is, not everyone is hearing the message in a way that is understandable and applicable. Some in the western world do not realize that many people, possibly up to two-thirds of the world's population, prefer a style of learning that leans away from the highly literate model often used in western contexts. One author notes that "we generally assume that people who hear our message should go on to read the Bible for themselves and thus be responsible for their own Christian development. Our plans to produce growing churches and mature Christians usually are dependent on studious, Bible-reading people" (Klem 1978: 479); but what do we do when we encounter those who cannot read?

The model Klem describes is often driven by printed Bible studies, discipleship curriculum, fill in the blank workbooks, and a host of Christian growth books. Klem assumes everyone wanted to learn to read when he began his work as a missionary. It was not until some years later that he realized "many of them did not want a religion that would require them to learn to read, because they valued personal, memorized, oral communication" (Klem 1978: 479). Such a statement carries far reaching implications. It seems that those Africans whom Klem ministered to equated Christianity with literacy. This equation caused some to reject the gospel because in their minds, it had become intertwined with foreign elements that were not desirable in their culture. Tom Steffen writes,

> "people's assumptions about God impact their perception of Scripture. Those who define the Supreme Being as a God of love often approach Scripture as devotional literature. People who view God as logical and linear often view the Bible as a book of verifiable propositions" (Steffen 2005: 1).

Steffen recounts that as a literate westerner he brought the same approach to ministry as that he had received. Steffen brought abstract systematic theology while his people wanted stories. He gave reasons; yet they wanted relationship. He gave categories; but they wanted characters. He gave explanation though they wanted exploration. He gave definitions while they wanted descriptions. Essentially, there was a big gap between Steffen's approach and what target audience was accustomed to before. Such is the case with many who immigrated to the U.S.

For the most part, the western approach to missions has involved a literate approach. Thomas finds a different picture in the Scriptures and writes, "God is a storytelling God. Deeper than this, God is the creator of story, and it is in the context of story that God calls us into mission" (Thomas 1999: 225). Modern missions practitioners are beginning to realize the truths of Scripture can be communicated in a variety of contextualized manners. Even the language used by missiologists is changing. Terms like "orality," Chronological Bible Storying," and "narrative theology" are much more common today in missions journals and books than fifty years ago.

This new vocabulary is a result of what Klem, Steffen, Thomas, and many others encountered oral learners on mission fields worldwide. Oral learners can simply be described as those who rely on spoken language for communication; rather than written. Orality is about much more than reading and writing, however. True oral people have a distinct approach to life played out through cognition, community, and communication that is very different from literate peoples. This section explores the oral worldview in general and will then examine the residual orality preference retained by many immigrants to North American cities.

The Oral Worldview

Orality is much more expansive than simply preferring to verbally communicate; rather than writing. Oral peoples approach life in a fundamentally different way than literate peoples. Such an approach to life is categorically called worldview. Worldview is the framework through which someone understands and interprets reality. It answers questions like what is possible in the world, how does the world work, and what are people fundamentally like? Whether the worldview is biblically accurate or not, to those people, perception *is* reality. Additionally, worldview is formed early in life and is difficult to change.

Oral peoples grow up in a society that is oriented to life differently than those growing up in a literate society. From the beginning of life, those nearest and dearest to an individual pass on the unique features of their culture. They share their stories of creation, cultural history, societal roles and relationships, and explain things like marriage, death, sickness, sin, and the spiritual world. People in the culture essentially teach the next generation what to think about life but also *how* to think about life. Oral peoples live life experientially and sometimes have trouble conceiving of ideas they have never personally experienced. Cognition in oral cultures is shaped by the physical and spiritual context the culture they live in.

Oral Language Structure

Oral peoples need to taste, feel, see, or use something in order for it to "exist." Words in and of themselves have no meaning and are only understood as occurrences and events in oral cultures (Ong 1982: 31). Anthropologist Claude Levi-Strauss concluded that for an oral person, something must be known or experienced to be real. He records oral peoples using precise words to distinguish subtleties of plants, animals, and weather phenomenon but he noticed that in most cases, the object being described is useful to the people. For example, chewing slightly narcotic nuts is an important cultural practice among the Hanunoo of the Philippines. The Hanunoo have words for four varieties of areca nut along with eight substitutes for that nut. Of the betel nut they speak of five varieties and five acceptable substitutes. Betel nut chewing is an important community experience in that culture and the Hanunoo have precise words to describe and distinguish sub-species of the plant. The Hanunoo have no distinct words for other fauna that is not useful, however. Though many other species of plant exist in the jungles surrounding their villages, the Hanunoo simply leave them unnamed or categorize them broadly under their generic word for plant (Levi-Strauss 1966: 2-3).

The northern Canadian Inuit language, Inuktitut, further illustrates an oral culture's preference for descriptive and functional words rather than abstract categories. A language informant pointed to a coffee cup on his desk and explained that in English, the word for the substance covering the cup is "enamel." He told me,

> "'Enamel' doesn't mean anything to us. The word doesn't tell us what the thing does. In Inuktitut, words describe the function of the thing rather than some abstract word like 'enamel' where the meaning must be filled in separate from the word." He went on to give several other examples including their word for "seal" which meant "that which comes up through the ice to breathe."

"Seal" by itself is an abstract word. The word does not bring an image to mind of a specific function in real life. The vocabulary of the language functioned according to the oral worldview of the Inuit, focusing on concrete and practical life experiences.

The approach of oral peoples to religion is also tied to their experience of god or the spirits acting in their lives. Thinking about God in an oral context is developed from an insider's perspective. Theology is applied and context based, answering the most important questions about life in that particular culture. Rather than being expressed in books, oral theology is stored in the mind and is delivered via community experience through dancing, singing, chanting, storytelling, poetry, and so on.

Categorization Process in Oral Cultures

There is a classic study on the cognitive processes of oral peoples that was conducted with oral peoples and those with very low levels of literacy in Uzbekistan in the former Soviet Union (Luria 1976). The findings, though perhaps overstated, provide insight into the experiential learning of oral peoples. Luria confirms that abstract categorization is a skill much more refined in literate societies than in oral ones. In the literate west, colors are intricately categorized and clearly distinct. "Red, yellow, orange, blue, green, black, white, and purple" are words used to separate colors that are more or less closely related. Luria believes that "the wealth of expressions for certain colors and the linguistic poverty of such terms for other colors result from differences in the practical importance that different colors have in different cultures" (Luria 1976: 23).

For example, many Arctic languages have dozens of terms for shades of white because each refers to a different type of snow or ice which is of vital practical importance in that culture. The ability to categorize various kinds of safe and unsafe ice conditions can mean the difference between life and death! The same language lacks any word for green because nothing of practical value in that region exists. Luria found that the Ichkari women he studied classified colored yarn according to what the color represented in their everyday life.

Unable to assign a general categorical color name, the women would say, "This is like calf's dung, and this is like a peach" (Luria 1976: 27).

One part of the study involved asking oral peoples to identify geometric figures like a circle, square, and triangle. Luria records in every instance, oral peoples named the figure as a representation of real objects they interacted with and never according to abstract categories like circle or square. Circles were identified as a plate, sieve, bucket, or moon. Even an incomplete circle was identified as a bracelet because of what it resembled. Triangles were called *tumar*, an Uzbek word for magical amulets, which are often designed in a way that looks like a triangle. Squares were called a door, house, or apricot drying board. Luria concludes that the oral people's "evaluation of abstract geometrical figures was decidedly concrete and object-oriented" (Luria 1976: 32-33).

A final test of oral cognition involved presenting four objects, three of which could be grouped together according to a taxonomic category or by their use in a practical situation. One set included a hammer, saw, ax, and log. The taxonomic category would group the tools together (hammer, saw, and ax) and exclude the log as a non-tool. Grouping the items according to practical value, the saw, ax, and log would go together and the hammer would be excluded because the hammer has no practical value to work the log. Luria found that the oral peoples he studied would group items according to their practical value for use in real life situations and not according to an abstract taxonomical category. Luria concludes

> The majority of our subjects were members of a society in which rudimentary practical functions constituted the fundamental human activity. Lacking the formal education that would have allowed for systematic intellectual development, these people regarded the logical procedures of categorization as irrelevant, of no practical value. Hence they substituted procedures that were more meaningful to them, analyzing an object according to its relevance to a functional situation. This approach took precedence over the verbal logical operations typical of abstract thinking (Luria 1976: 98).

Luria may have overstated his case in some instances and unfairly drew too hard a line between the abilities of literate and non-literate peoples. However, what is clear is that such a practical approach to cognition, rejecting abstract categorization, and operating according to tangible objects in the culture has massive implications for how missionaries might present the gospel. Many times, the approach to evangelism a missionary uses includes referring to abstract categories like holiness, sin, forgiveness, and so on. Missionaries must learn how to present the gospel in a tangible way that meshes with the oral cognition process, and is directly applicable to the daily life of the people.

Memory in Oral Cultures

I have heard many times from missionaries that the memories of oral peoples are astounding. They can hear a Bible story once and have it memorized verbatim. However, is it possible that even memory itself functions differently in an oral culture? In a literate culture, verbatim memorization is valued and is possible because a message can be checked against a written text continually until total accuracy is achieved. Ong notes that historically, many literate researchers wrongly assumed that oral people must also value verbatim memory. He suggests that "literates were happy simply to assume that the prodigious oral memory functioned somehow according to their own verbatim textual model" (Ong 1982: 58). Once means to record and analyze oral deliveries were available, researchers discovered that in many cases, verbatim memory actually did not happen. In fact, such precise memory was not even expected or attempted by oral peoples.

Some of the greatest works of literature are Homer's *Iliad* and *Odyssey*. For many years, these works were thought to have been written down by Homer, but in depth studies on their poetic structure have revealed that they were almost certainly oral works that were memorized (Parry 1971). These poems were found to be carefully arranged in strict metrical patterns. Parry discovered that the hexameters were not just word units based on their respective syllables. Rather, Homer had arranged the works based on common formulas that contained the same groups of words every time. These word groups served to introduce segments of the poems, similar to an acrostic, so all that had to be memorized were the word groups that were already made into the correct metrical structure for the poem. Homer was then free to slightly alter the actual content for each section of the poem and not change the overall structure or storyline. Key characters were assigned characteristics such as "clever Odysseus" to remind Homer of the plot of that particular segment of the poem. In summary, Parry's extensive study of Homeric poetry revealed that it was not necessary for Homer to have memorized the poem verbatim in order to tell it with reasonable accuracy.

Parry's understudy, Albert Lord, continued Parry's work with Homeric poetry but also tested modern epic oral poets to attempt to confirm the hypothesis that these poets did not memorize their stories verbatim; but rather memorized thematically. Lord studied Yugoslavic oral poets who also used a metrically governed, formulaic style to compose their works. He recorded the bards' songs and found that, though they were metrically and thematically the same, they were never sung the exact same way twice. Lord concludes that the memory feats of these singers are remarkable, but are unlike the kind of memory that is expected from those with a written text.

Interestingly, the singers themselves think they are singing the same song or reciting the poem verbatim but they are not. Lord records a conversation with a poet where the poet continually affirms that he can memorize a new song right away and sing it without changing a word. He even swears by Allah that it is not good to add or take away from a song.

However, when the poet is recorded singing the song several times, it is easily discovered that he does indeed change the wording every time. He just does not realize he is doing so because oral peoples do not think of memorization as having to be verbatim. To them, thematic memorization is the only kind they know (Lord 1964: 26-28). Lord notes that literates often think of memorization of a poem as needing to be "word for word and line for line." However, these oral poets do not know what "words" or "lines" are. Goody has identified oral languages that often have a word for speech in general, or for a rhythmic unit in a poem or song, or for a theme, but have no word for "word" as in an isolated and singular bit of speech (Goody 1977: 115).

Ong adds that the "sense of individual words as significantly discrete items is fostered by writing" (Ong 1982: 61). Since the concept of "words" does not exist in the oral mind, word for word and line for line memorization simply mean "alike," but not "exactly alike" as a literate person might define word for word memorization. Such an approach to memory must be considered when introducing the Bible to oral peoples. Should the missionary expect word for word memorization of the Scripture or Bible story? Does the oral person have liberty to slightly alter the message when he retells the story? An ignorant understanding of how oral memory works may lead to a false sense of security regarding the abilities of oral peoples to remember Bible stories over time, especially when these stories are told by a missionary or church planter through a translator.

The Importance of Community in Oral Cultures

The presence of the local community is much more important in oral cultures than in literate cultures. In many cases, known local leaders carry the authority in the community in contrast to literate cultures where authority often rests with unknown government officials or books written by Ph.D.: holding experts that have no relationship with anyone in the local community. Thomas Boomershine notes that the root meaning of the word authority comes from the word author. He reasons that the authority of the Scriptures is based on their author, God (Boomershine 1988: 20). Drawing out Boomershine's thought, the source of authority in an oral culture is tied to the author or speaker in that community. The written word, on the other hand, separates the original communicator from those who eventually receive the message. In an oral culture, "learning or knowing means achieving close, empathetic, communal identification with the known [the originator of the information]" (Havelock 1963: 145-46).

In contrast, the mindset of western literates commonly found over the past two centuries is that if anything is truly important, it must be in writing, documented, signed, and sealed. According to this mindset, no merely oral word can carry the kind of legal, scholarly, or administrative authority compared to what a written and published document can. Western missions practitioners historically came from cultures steeped in written history. Graham states that it is difficult to overemphasize the perceived significance of writing. Noted authorities in years past have made statements along the lines that purely oral communication is unable to provide for progressive cultural development and that only writing can bridge a man from the tribal to the civilized realm (Ong 1982: 12). Official papers with signatures of those in positions of authority are common in literate societies. The authority resides not in the document or in the one bringing the document but in the one whom the signature represents. Such external sources of authority and enforcement are not as powerful or respected in an oral culture.

Community Control of Message: Transmission and Acceptance

The oral community itself serves as the enforcement agency for accuracy in oral communication. Many oral communities use a system called the informal, controlled oral tradition. Within this tradition, there are three levels of community control and expectation enforced on the material transmitted. In some cases, there is little control and total flexibility in the message. An example is telling a joke. The general flow and punch line remain the same but characters may be altered to fit the context. At the other end, the community exerts near total control and the message is allowed little to no flexibility.

An example is an epic poem or proverb key to the identity of the culture. In the middle is a method allowing for some flexibility and interpretation, but still falling under the control of the community at large. Parables, stories, and historical narratives fall within this arena, with the community controlling conformity of the message in general, but allowing for slight changes with regard to characters or specific incidents depicted in the story. The method of transmission and control are the most common in oral societies, as will be shown below.

The oral community expresses itself in a personal and contextual way. One author notes

> The theology of the oral Church is automatically more pragmatic, more experiential, less critical, less logical, and more personal. It relies, if you will, more on testimony, and less on written texts. Written texts – even the Bible itself – are judged according to this different set of expectations, and they play a fundamentally different role in the daily life of the Church than they do in the technical world of scholarship (Camery-Hoggatt 2005: 249).

Oral theology in the context described above requires a community because the people's expression of theology is personal to their tribe and is closely tied to the perceived ways God has worked in their lives. The more distant from the people the messenger is, the less likely the message will be received.

The community aspect of oral cultures informs how they approach and understand "truth" as well. In fact, in oral cultures "truth" might be understood as relationship plus experience. If an oral person has not experienced the phenomenon himself or does not have a close relationship with someone who has experienced it, the idea may not be seen as true or possible. An understanding of truth, even the truth of the Scriptures often involves the entire community or body of believers in the culture. The presence of a local prominent societal figure or gatekeeper plays a crucial role in the community's willingness to accept new information as true. The relationship of the community with the teacher or speaker is as important as the actual features of the message itself. Consider the following example:

> Just as oral people distrust experts, so also oral Christians tend to measure theological competence against a more pragmatic yardstick. Consider this comment, which I once overheard at an Assembly of God district council: "He may have a string of degrees, but he can't preach his way out of a paper bag." What matters here is not what is said, but the assumption upon which the claim is made: The ability to preach one's way out of a paper bag is surely more important than a Ph.D behind one's name. In an oral community, "them as can, does; them as can't teaches." Practice trumps theory every time. It is not that the experts know something that the oral preacher cannot find out. It is that that expert knows something the oral preacher thinks is irrelevant (Camery-Hoggatt 2005: 248).

Oral cultures "demonstrate a certain pattern of thought and behavior. Characteristics of such cultures include lack of concern for original forms and authorship, extreme respect for rhetorical skills, placing greater value on interpersonal interaction than on abstract sets of values and logical deductions, and stress on the community rather than on individualism and individual thought" (Davis 2008: 754). When Davis refers to original forms and authorship, he is referring to outside forms and authors. Authority in an oral society does not come from the outside, no matter how reputable that individual may be. When introducing new information, the connection between the knower and the known is crucial. Again, the community aspect of understanding truth is crucial for those ministering in oral contexts. If the missionary is seen as an outsider, the message carries much less weight than it might otherwise.

Oral Communication Methods

In an oral culture, "voice" is more than just an audible frequency. Speech is created and clothed by the speaker, dressed to fit the occasion. In contrast to print communication, "The genuineness or shallowness of the [message] is communicated by a speaker in inflection, tears, smiles, rhythm, cadence, and intensity. Books don't do that" (Sheard 2007: 21, 24). Furthermore, oral communication conveys para-messages such as tone, gesture, and spatial distance – all things that "speak" as clearly as words do. Oral peoples use delivery mechanisms like proverbs, parables, and stories that do not just supplement a logical argument as in a western sermon, but are the very storehouses that contain knowledge in an oral society.

In this way, the people own their speech in a way unique to oral peoples. Klem provides an example of this kind of speech ownership. He had been using recorded Bible stories with a Yoruba tribe, coming each week to share the message with the people. One day, a local man challenged Klem to a test of ownership of the message on the tapes; the man who could sing the largest portion of the message from memory was allowed to stay and keep the message. The one who could sing the least had to stand at a distance. Klem records that such oral communication feats were the indigenous method of proving cultural ownership of knowledge. The Yoruba man boasted that only a wise man could compose and sing that kind of poetry (Klem 1995: 63-64).

Many missionaries and church planters are familiar with oral cultures' traditions of storying. Oral peoples will often explain their entire heritage, values, religious system, and education model through stories. In fact, N.T. Wright notes that every worldview is made up of stories that explain origins and reality. These stories function like bricks in a foundation that builds the worldview of the people. Bible Storying is a method used to share biblical truth in a format already present in an oral culture. The stories are carefully chosen from the Bible and are told with the hopes that they will replace the "bricks" of the false worldview of the people. A detailed approach to Bible storying is explained in Chapter 7.

Oral cultures use rituals as a prime communication mechanism as well. Rituals are community dramas that are regularly repeated and communicate deep beliefs, feelings, and values of the people. In animistic oral cultures, rituals connect the people with the spirit world and give added sincerity to the message because in oral cultures, words divorced from a known context have no value. The ritual adds context to the communication. One type of ritual is a rite of passage. Bruce Olson encountered such a situation with the Motilones in Columbia where the people had great "sing-offs" that a boy must participate in to enter manhood. A youth would spend an entire night reciting the people's cultural history through song and would never be viewed as a boy again (Olson 1995: 144-45).

Westerners have historically been afraid of rituals and often are anti-ritual. Not knowing how to handle rituals in a culture, they would often ban all local rituals in churches they planted. The problem with this approach is multi-faceted. First, the missionaries rarely had any understanding of the purpose of the ritual. To the people, the rite of passage was the *only* way for a boy to enter manhood. Without the ritual, the entire community continually viewed the boy as, well, a boy who was not allowed to marry or become a warrior. In some African cultures, all drumming was banned because missionaries thought it was always associated with demonic activity. They did not realize that only some drumming patterns were used to call up the spirits and by banning all drumming, they robbed the culture of a key communication element. True, some rituals are always associated with the demonic and must be put away. But, many rituals are biblically permissible or can remain with only slight modification. The point is that rituals are an important communication means in oral cultures. Rituals can tell a story central to the realities of life for the people. The Story can become their story. In fact, "oral learners 'enter' the story and as they absorb sensory data they live the story in the present tense – seeing, hearing, tasting, smelling and feeling what the persons in the story are experiencing" (Claydon 2005: 22).

Additional communication means such as drama and dance are common in oral cultures. In some Asian cultures, certain forms of drama are a primary means to communicate religious and cultural values. In China, music was thought to have a power of its own and Confucian and Taoist teachings were common themes in Chinese opera. Similarly, in India, dance and drama are used to communicate the Jataka Tales, or birth stories about the Buddha (Hesselgrave 1991: 550). These art forms are more than mere entertainment. They are used to shape and reinforce the worldview of the people, bringing together the seen and unseen worlds and explaining the mysteries of origin, birth, sickness, death, good, evil, truth, and beauty (Ray 1971: 8). Even after the introduction of literacy, these oral communication methods still prevail. For example, Chinese immigrants to cities in Malaysia bring their dance and theatre traditions. Chinese street opera is commonly found and often feature classics such as Romance of the Three Kingdoms, The Water Margin, and Madam White Snake (Koh and Ho 2009: 64).

The Lomwe of Africa house their theology in their songs, not in written texts as literates might. Laryea writes of "the many ordinary Christians whose reflections on the gospel can be discerned in their prayers, songs, testimonies, thank offerings, and sermons. They are the ones who are now beginning to set for us the parameters and framework for doing theology in a new key" (Quoted in Foster 2008: 130). Laryea recorded and analyzed two-hundred sixty three songs to discern the theology of the tribe. Themes that emerged were deemed most important and found to be most contextual to the people. Prominent themes were judgment, the return of Christ, sins, repentance, death, and life described as a journey. These Lomwe songs were developed in the community of the tribe and were direct expressions of their understanding of God. This is an example of the power of indigenous song writing as a means to teach theology in an oral culture.

Finally, oral peoples often use proverbs and stories to communicate deep cultural truths. Proverbs are short, pithy statements that are often the "hanger" for a complex series of beliefs that the proverb illustrates. In the U.S., for example, we might say "time is money." What do those three words signify? They signify an entire cultural understanding of time as a "commodity" that can be purchased, used, and wasted. So, in business, if we are "wasting" time, we are wasting money. A manager might walk through the floor and spot a worker talking too long with another co-worker. All the manager has to do is walk by and say "time is money" and the employee will fill the proverb with culturally derived meaning, take it as a rebuke, end the conversation, and get back to "work." Such thinking is culturally determined and many cultures around the world do not see time as a commodity that can be wasted so the proverb "time is money" would have no applicable meaning. The point is that every culture has many proverbs that function in this way – a few memorable words that carry deep cultural values and truths. Church planters would do well to learn the proverbs of the target people and use them as bridges to the gospel or as "hangers" which to attach Bible stories or biblical teaching. Oral peoples are adept at storing the teaching under the hanger of the proverb and the recitation of the proverb will bring to mind the entire teaching which the proverb summarizes – like a sort of library retrieval mechanism.

Introduction of Literacy

I have labored to describe the intricacies of a purely oral worldview because, as Ong states, "A deeper understanding of pristine or primary orality enables us better to understand the new world of writing, what it truly is, and what functionally literate human beings really are" (Ong 1982: 78). Introducing literacy to an oral people involves much more than simply teaching them to read. The shift often requires an upheaval of society. Hiebert explains that even something as seemingly innocuous as a written calendar can have far reaching consequences. The calendar introduces days, weeks, months, and years that often do not match the seasons or agrarian lifestyle of many oral peoples. The solar and lunar solstices no longer govern the year, rather, marks on a paper now tell people what to do and when to do it (Hiebert 2008: 138-39). So, do not be surprised when your new immigrant friends do not seem to respect your calendar driven schedule and pay no attention to "clock time."

Additionally, the printed word disconnects ideas and information from a known source. The message of a book is no longer connected with village leaders who hold real and perceived authority. There is no immediate context for the passing of written information. Further, writing requires interpretation since the speaker is not present to explain him or herself. As noted above, oral cultures prefer a communal interpretation process tied to a local and known authority. Books written by highly educated experts carry little weight because context and relationship are so important for an oral culture to accept something as true.

Books require a move away from this centralized authority present in oral cultures. Those bringing knowledge are now outside of the culture, have no relationship to the people, cannot defend their argument, and have little weight in the culture. If outside authorities like authors of books are seen as foreign to the ways of the oral culture, there is a higher likelihood that the new information will be dismissed. I remember preaching in a rural church in Kentucky many years ago. I was taught to back up my sermons and Bible interpretation by citing credible authors and commentaries. I began to notice that when the main pastor (a local boy) preached, he would use a different approach to add credibility to his message. When he was about to say something important, he would lean over the pulpit and in a low voice say "you know me, I'm just an 'ol boy from down the road. I grew up in these parts…." and then would go on to make his point. It used to drive me crazy until I realized he was actually a genius! He was identifying himself with the community, as one of them, and in turn, gained tremendous credibility that I never had.

Orality – Literacy Spectrum

All peoples in the world fall on a spectrum between primary orality and highly literate. A description of the spectrum is helpful, especially for those working with immigrants from oral backgrounds.   Many have a tendency to over generalize the nature of oral cultures and place anything related to orality under the category of primary oral learner. Such a generalization is unhelpful. Primary oral learners occupy an extreme end of the literacy spectrum. Those living in this culture have little to no exposure to print materials. The spoken language may not have been reduced to writing at all. Primary oral cultures house all of their cultural knowledge in their minds. Information is delivered through speaking, singing, dancing, proverbs, oral poetry, and art simply because no other media exists to transmit information.

Further along the literacy spectrum is the secondary oral culture. The written word is familiar to those in this culture but is not the preferred means of communication. People may know how to read but may not have read a book since elementary school. Those in a secondary oral culture may use writing on occasion, such as for legal documents, but information is usually transmitted via story, poem, or song. Many of the unreached people groups today are secondary oral learners.

Closer to the literate end of the spectrum are the residual oral learners. These people use reading and writing every day. Written historical records may exist chronicling their culture. Literacy is familiar and common. However, the deepest cultural values may still be communicated orally through epic poems, songs, or ritual dances. Additionally, residual oral learners may still place a higher value on knowledge and "truth" coming from known sources rather than from unknown "experts." For example, I once was sharing with a co-worker that my son was well behind in language development according to pediatricians. We had just given an assessment exam to my son to see if he would qualify for a state speech assistance program. My coworker was not convinced by any of these professional studies and instead said to me, "Your boy will be fine. I have a friend whose son had similar problems but everything worked out." To my coworker, there was more credibility in her friend's experience than in scientific studies produced by unknown "experts!" It takes a long time for a culture to completely move away from its oral roots and many times, residual oral learners still give more authority to new information coming from someone they already have a relationship with.

Finally, there is the highly literate end of the spectrum where the preferred medium for communication is the written word. People are more comfortable writing an essay about a topic than acting it out through a drama. The vast majority of learning takes place through reading and little cultural history is stored in oral form. Few people in the culture can recite their history without first brushing up through reading. Few people in the world fall into the highly literate category.

Since people fall somewhere on this spectrum, there can be no one size fits all approach to ministry. Some strategies take approaches intended for primary oral learners and use them in all situations. Immigrants to North America bring their culture with them, including their learning preferences. Many enroll in ESL classes after arrival in this country. As noted above, though they may know how to read, oftentimes, secondary oral learners still prefer an oral method of communication for things most dear to them like cultural values and religious beliefs. An orality assessment tool is included in the appendix of this book and is explained in more detail in Chapter 6. Church planters would be wise to use the tool to gauge the appropriate level of orality strategies to use in church planting and discipleship.

Summary

Church planting in general is hard work; but church planting among immigrant ethnic peoples is compounded by linguistic, cultural, and learning style differences. This chapter has shown that it is not as simple as taking church planting strategies from the North American context and importing them to reach ethnic peoples; as Paul Hiebert noted that this approach is bound for failure. Ethnic church planting is not impossible, however, so be not despair! The next chapters of this book are written to give you the tools to understand and develop appropriate strategies for reaching ethnic peoples with the gospel.

PART 3

UNDERSTANDING AND IDENTIFYING ETHNIC GROUPS IN THE CITY

CHAPTER 5

ASSIMILATION THEORY AND PATTERNS

Introduction

Immigration has been occurring in the United States since, well, before the United States were united. U.S. cities came into their own in the later 19th and early 20th centuries. Urban studies in the U.S. have their roots in the University of Chicago, which houses the first sociology department in an American university. Robert Park was one of the school's first faculty and transitioned to teaching from a background in journalism. Park had been particularly interested in issues of race and crime in urban contexts and found the city of Chicago an ideal laboratory for study. Later, other urban researchers began studying how social networks produced communities in the city. These scholars focused on micro communities that function within the larger urban center. Essentially, they reduced the city to the individual neighborhood, where local identity became the grounding feature of living in a diverse urban environment.

Current anthropological study realizes that cities are complex and interconnected. It is no longer possible to study people or neighborhoods in the city in isolation (Rynkiewich 2011). Globalization, transnationalism, and the internet mean that people are connected in many layers, have many social networks, and influence and are influenced by people and trends well outside of their individual neighborhood. These modern trends impact how immigrants interact with their own people, but also how they interact with mainstream society. Our approach to understanding immigration and ethnic identity in the city must change as the world globalizes. Anthropologist Darrell Whiteman writes "we have often been more comfortable as 'bush anthropologists' stomping through the steaming jungle than we are trying to make . . . sense out of the concrete jungle of today's megacities, teeming with a diversity of cultures, religions, and economic classes" (Whiteman 2006: 53). People from diverse backgrounds come to the U.S. and seek to survive and thrive. They must come up with some strategy to survive, even as they navigate assimilation with mainstream culture.

Assimilation Theory Throughout the 20th Century

Assimilation is a complicated and contested idea. One only has to think of the metaphors used to describe the cultural climate in the U.S. to understand the conflicting ideas of how assimilation works: the melting pot, stew, salad, or tapestry. Each image illustrates a theory of the level to which immigrants assimilate into mainstream culture. Assimilation is important for church planting because we need to know how much of the original language and culture immigrants retain. If we are trying to reach Cambodians in California, we need to know if Buddhist values still play out in their thinking, family structure, group cohesion, and decision making.

Early assimilation theory suggested that assimilation was entirely one sided – immigrants would inevitably melt into mainstream American culture. People thought that immigrants were to discard their cultural identities as inferior in favor of acquiring superior mainstream American cultural values. This idea smacks of ethnocentrism – placing your own culture at the center and judging others by it. This thinking was strong around World War 2 as western military might and technological advancement were confused with cultural superiority. Here, immigrants must "play the game by our rules or leave." The cultural standard was the White, Anglo-Saxon, Protestant (WASP) model popularized in the book *Assimilation in American Life* (Gordon 1964). Western Europeans were the ideal immigrants because they could quickly "melt" into mainstream culture and no one would know the difference. Darker skinned immigrants and longtime African Americans were viewed as incompletely assimilating, even as they were asked to essentially become white Americans.

Over time, this "assimilate or perish" mentality fell away as immigrant peoples maintained their cultural characteristics and still found success in America. The multi-cultural mentality arose, where ethnic groups could maintain their distinct ethnic identity in the midst of surrounding diversity. The rise of ethnic enclaves like Chinatowns in San Francisco and New York provided grounds for a vigorous ethnic cohesion where groups were free to express their ethnic identity. However, overtime, ethnic enclaves have dwindled and many immigrants today live in the suburbs, perhaps miles from someone else from their same ethnic group.

The best way to understand assimilation is to view it as a two way endeavor where, yes, mainstream culture impacts immigrants, but immigrants also impact mainstream culture. One only has to survey the city today to see the dramatic impact immigrant groups have had on mainstream American culture. The popularity of ethnic restaurants has skyrocketed among white Americans. Major universities have more Asians in local Christian ministries and more whites in Buddhist campus groups than ever before. Bikram and other forms of yoga are popular all over the U.S., and are often taught by white instructors trained overseas or in one of the many local schools such as the Bikram Yoga College of India in San Diego, CA.

Ethnic communities are not passive recipients of the culture around them. They certainly impact mainstream culture as well. Assimilation is a two way endeavor that needs a balanced understanding which requires neither complete assimilation into some faceless romanticized "American" culture, nor does it romanticize ethnic pluralism in the form of isolated ethnically segregated enclave communities oblivious to the surrounding city.

Metaphors of the City: Divided, Contested, and Stabilized

In many ways, characteristics of cities are difficult to generalize. Some say that global cities have more in common with each other than they do with their surrounding country. This may be true, but cities in the U.S. vary greatly in their feel, make up, and characteristics. We have declining cities like Detroit and Pittsburgh. We have east coast cities like Boston, Philadelphia, and New York. We have west coast cities like Los Angeles, San Francisco, Portland, and Seattle. We have gentile southern cities like Birmingham. We have cities isolated in farm country like Champagne-Urbana, Illinois. Each of these cities has different industries, different economies, and different flavors. However, most U.S. cities share three common metaphoristic features – they are divided, contested, and yet act as a stabilizing force on their residents (Low 1999).

The Divided City

The divided city metaphor brings to mind images of living on the "wrong side of the tracks" or the "bad side of town." Cities do indeed have these physical divisions. In recent years a phenomenon known as gentrification is causing new division in urban centers. Gentrification refers to a kind of renewal of dilapidated neighborhoods flowing from an influx of money and cultural investment to areas previously abandoned by the largely white middle and upper class. Now, old warehouses become art centers and project housing is torn down and modernist condos are built. There is an old slaughterhouse in Louisville's Butchertown neighborhood (catchy, right?) that is now a trendy art studio where hundreds of artists rent space to create everything from paintings to chainsaw tree art. Nearby, old dive bars are now called "gastropubs" and what were once $1.50 beers now sell for $5 and craft cocktails costing over $10 are the rage. One characteristic of gentrification is the old, lower class is driven out as property values and the general cost of living increase as the neighborhood gentrifies and poor people can no longer afford to live in their own neighborhood.

Other cities have great gated communities where the wealthy live. One cannot enter this divided section of the city without certain credentials. Once inside, the elite no longer have to worry about the crime, dirt, busyness, and noise common in the rest of the city. Within the walls of these communities lay all that is needed to enjoy life. Grocery stores, auto service centers, hair salons, and even places of worship fill the space within the gated area of the city. This type of urban planning speaks a message: the poor and undesirables are not welcome. There need be no mixing of class in the divided city. For example, in London, I discovered that many white Brits prefer to drive their own cars and do not use the "Tube" or the subway because they see it as a place for poor immigrants who cannot afford their own cars or the gas to operate them.

Cities like Chicago and Los Angeles each contain more than seventy distinct neighborhood communities, many of which are markedly mono-ethnic. A single street separates Hispanics from Greeks, blacks from South Asians. There is little crossing over. The prominence of gangs protecting their territory and the informal economies of drugs, prostitutes, and stolen goods lead to further division of groups. I was once walking to a ministry site on the south side of Chicago when a bold 10 year old African-American kid confronted me and said, "Man, why you gotta come to my neighborhood? Go back to your neighborhood where you belong!" This kid knew from experience that white people didn't "belong" in his area of town and that perception really shaped his interaction with outsiders.

Furthermore, local government coding and low income housing laws segregate many immigrants. Refugees in particular cannot just live wherever they want, at least initially. Certain apartment complexes in Louisville are known for housing refugees. The government partners with these apartments to funnel newly arriving refugees for initial settlement. Many of these complexes are in bad shape and ridden by crime and violence. Sometimes, ethnic groups themselves further divide the city by purchasing old buildings like the Somalis have in Louisville. The Somali Mall, as it's called, contains everything a Somali needs to survive – there is a mosque, coffee shop, cafeteria, grocery store, tax preparation center, and dozens of stalls selling everything from clothing to household goods. Such division promotes a lack of need to assimilate into the surrounding culture. A Somali refugee need not learn English because he can have all needs met inside the mall.

The ultimate expression of ethnic division within a city is the ethnic enclave like various Chinatowns, Little Havana, Little Italy, and so on. Generally, enclaves are geographically bounded and ethnically cohesive and contain their own economies, religious, and cultural centers in the midst of a diverse city. In some cases, these groups so dominate their territory that newly arriving immigrants do not need to learn English to find work for the rest of their lives.

The Contested City

Division within a city, both physically and ethnically, leads to the contested city. I remember walking the streets of the Ozone Park neighborhood in Queens and asking "whose neighborhood is this, anyway?" I saw Jamaicans, Latinos, and Bengalis all fighting for ownership of the area. Each group wanted ethnic dominance so they could corner the market to rent shop space, sell more of their own goods, and draw a larger customer base. New York City only issues so many street vendor food permits and there are only so many good locations to sell at. The Bengalis wanted to dominate this market and push out competition. While researching in London I came across the Seven Sisters Market, a large open air market with rental stalls for selling goods. The market was locally known as the Latino market because so many immigrants from Ecuador and Peru rented stalls and sold goods there. Or so we thought. I came across a Chinese vendor and asked her what she thought of the Latino market. She adamantly denied that it was a Latino market and stated it was the Seven Sisters Market. She was voicing her right to belong as a minority in the midst of an ethnically dominated space.

The contested city leads to an ingroup/outgroup mentality as different groups vie for power. Usually, ethnic groups fight to establish a hierarchy which governs neighborhoods. There are dominant and minority groups, and how these groups relate to each other and to outsiders can make the difference between receptivity of the gospel or hostility toward it. Church planters must begin where people are, not where they want them to be, and in multi-ethnic urban neighborhoods, it is essential they have the tools to understand the relational dynamics at play.

Minority peoples and immigrants are often most aware of their ethnic consciousness and feel the subtle racism and discrimination that those in the dominant group rarely notice. Coming from the majority culture in the U.S., I (Anthony) was not aware of the degree of suspicion projected toward African-Americans until I spent a summer in Chicago and heard stories of dark skinned people who were avoided on the streets and closely monitored whenever they entered the store of a white owner. These kinds of cultural clashes often arise from a lack of relationship with people of a different race or ethnicity. The unknown breeds fear, anxiety, and stereotypes. Stereotypes are a kind of cultural shortcut – you don't actually need to get to know somebody when you can blanket categorize them according to a stereotype. Mark Twain once said that travel is the best cure for prejudice. He is largely correct. Getting to know someone who is different than you reduces anxiety of the unknown and humanizes people from an abstract "ethnic group." I remember the first time a Muslim man held my helpless infant child. It was in that moment that I realized more fully that Muslims are people too. That may seem harsh, but it is all too easy to label someone a "Muslim" and never know them as a person whom God made and loves.

The point is that in ethnically contested spaces, there are a host of factors at work that bar people from interacting with each other. These factors may be economic competition, gang territory, ugly stereotypes, or some historical issue with lasting consequences. Minority peoples usually do not feel comfortable in the same territory as the majority culture, especially if there is a history of discrimination. So, in the Seven Sisters market in London, church planters should not expect to reach Asians by hosting a Bible study or storying group in a Latino market stall. The hostility between the dominant and minority groups is simply too strong.

The City as Stabilizer

What do we do with the contested city? Ethnic individuals and groups now live in a heterogeneous cultural environment, often very different from the mono-cultural tribal villages from which they immigrated. The city forces contact with "the other," people not like you. This forced contact "transforms migrant groups into ethnic communities with shared memories and perceptions, because it is on the city streets that migrants discover their own similarities in opposition to the world around them" (Portes 1995: 257). Sometimes, immigration intensifies ethnic identity as groups bind tightly together for a sense of community in a threatening world. Other times, immigrants seek to adopt and integrate into mainstream culture as a means of survival. Either way, groups and individuals must figure out how to get along with each other. In that sense, the city acts as a stabilizer.

The city and its ethnic groups have a dynamic relationship and one of continual renegotiation as urban culture, traditions, economic viability, and use of physical space change with the flux of incoming and outgoing peoples and changing city zoning laws. Immigrants navigate these changes as they come up with assimilation and integration strategies that work best for their families and people. Immigrants respond to the pressures of cultural heterogeneity in one of three broad patterns. Some immigrants choose to form or are forced to form tightknit ethnic enclaves such as a Chinatown, Little Italy, or Little Havana. Other groups do not live in an enclave community but maintain close ties to their people through social networks spread throughout a geographic dispersion in the city. Still others leave behind many of their own cultural preferences and identity and band together into an urban "tribe" centered around a uniting affinity that plays a larger role than their own individual cultural heritage. Each assimilation pattern carries unique characteristics and requires a different strategy for church planting.

Background Factors Determining Assimilation Strategy

Immigrants face many choices as they adapt to life in the United States. Strategies are formed, usually with the second, third, or even future generations in mind. First generation immigrants ask what will be best in the long term? Generally, two main strategies for economic viability are possible, depending of what skills and background the immigrant possesses. First, there is the "ethnic" strategy which relies on the social network of the immigrant. Second, there is the "mainstream" strategy where the immigrant enrolls children in the American educational system, learns English, and enters the mainstream economy. These two basic strategies are often dependent on a theory known as forms of capital, which divides into two forms – human capital and social capital.

Human Capital

Human capital is a concept used in the social sciences and refers to a person's high level of education and professional work experience. Immigrants with high levels of human capital tend to be professionals and live in the middle class or above in their home countries. They have college degrees at least, and many have masters and doctorates as well. These immigrants migrate as families because they have the means to do so. They often seek permanent settlement in the new country, take a long term perspective on life, and seek to re-establish their middle and upper-class lifestyle. Often, they live in the suburbs of major cities. They bring money and skills that allow them to assimilate into mainstream culture if they wish. They avoid ethnic enclaves because they want their children to have the best education, learn English well, and successfully enter the mainstream economy. They are the doctors, lawyers, and engineers establishing the foundation of many institutions in the United States. I met a number of Indian and Pakistani Muslims at a mosque in Cincinnati, Ohio who were doctors at hospitals in Cincinnati and Dayton. They saw themselves first as Americans and secondly as Muslims. They were striving for a high level of assimilation, but one that did not completely absorb their cultural identity.

Asian immigrants tend to compose the majority of those immigrating with high levels of human capital. Two subgroups would be Filipinos and South Asian Indians. Many of my doctors growing up were Filipinos. These groups come from countries where English is widely spoken and education opportunities are numerous. A third subgroup of Asian human capital immigrants are Koreans. Koreans often do not speak fluent English prior to arrival but bring high levels of financial capital and business savvy. Koreans typically invest in small businesses and are good at bridging the gap between a Korean driven ethnic economy and the mainstream American economy. I have

51

a friend who started a gas station distribution business. Basically, he provides everything you can buy at a gas station except the gasoline. My friend did not speak fluent English when he arrived, but implemented a number of go-betweens so he could manage the finances of the business and still negotiate relationships with his clients. Increasingly, as English is taught more widely, Chinese immigrants are comprising a larger percentage of those coming with human capital. Groups with human capital usually raise children that excel in school, earn professional and graduate degrees, and marry outside their ethnic group.

Social Capital

Social capital is the contrasting counterpart to human capital. Those possessing social capital are primarily labor migrants. They lack education and technical skills – human capital.   However, they are in touch with vast networks of social relationships that span the gap from their small home villages to larger gateway cities where they leave their home country and then on to their destination in the U.S. These immigrants rely on word of mouth as to the right time to migrate, how to navigate a border crossing, finding that first job, and getting by in the U.S. I am not implying that all immigrants with social capital are illegal, but many immigrants who are illegal also fall into the social capital category. This reliance on social networks produces a dependence on those who have gone before them. These workers are more likely to be exploited, earn low wages, and have little opportunity for advancement. They are not as likely to stay long term in the U.S. as those coming with high levels of human capital. In cities, these immigrants often live in enclave communities where they do not need to learn English and their possible illegal status can be overlooked when applying for a job.

Social capital immigrants primarily come from Mexico and other Central American countries, the Caribbean basin, and a smaller stream from China. It generally takes longer for these immigrants and their children to assimilate and join the mainstream economy. If the second generation only attains a high school diploma, their education has already far exceeded that of their parents. Dropout rates in school are high. Additionally, the reliance on social networking and the enclave environment often means living in hostile areas with higher levels of gangs and violence as groups fight for economic and political power in the enclave environment.

In summary, the forms of capital theory is helpful for church planters to understand because it can be used to predict patterns of assimilation, longevity of residence, and interaction of peoples from around the world. Immigrants with high levels of human capital coming from educated, professional backgrounds have the ability to choose where they live and are often dispersed throughout the city or in the suburbs. They are more likely to remain long term in the U.S. and are less likely to be dependent on their social networks in order to come to the States. On the other hand, those with high levels of social capital are more likely to live in ethnic enclaves, learn little English, and return to their home countries. Their family and social ties should be much more important to them, sometimes to the point where they become obligated to unintended roles in the new community. Immigrants from each of these forms of capital backgrounds tend to assimilate into one of three general patterns, each with its own unique characteristics.

Three Models of Immigrant Assimilation

In broad strokes, assimilation strategy takes on three major forms. First, ethnic enclaves form where an ethnic group is bound in a dense geographic location. Enclaves contain the least amount of assimilation, as least with regard to the ethnic group moving toward the mainstream culture. Second, some immigrants do not group geographically in an enclave, but they form tight social networks among themselves that function like cultural threads linking them together over a dispersed geographic area. Third, the urban tribe mentality requires the most among of assimilation as individuals from multiple groups drops aspects of their culture and form a distinct, new cultural identity. This new group is composed of highly heterogeneous individuals living as a group in the mainstream urban culture or sub-culture of the city.

Ethnic Enclaves[14]

Enclaves may be the most prominent image that comes to mind when most Americans think of immigrant groups. In general terms, an enclave can by any form of immigrant concentration within a loose geographic boundary. Technically, true enclaves need also to have an economic component as well that is run by and is for members of that ethnic group. A true enclave is both defined geographically and economically. For example, there is a small Somali enclave in Louisville. Somali refugees have banded together and bought an old warehouse that is now called the Somali Mall. Within the warehouse, one can find dozens of rooms and stalls housing everything from a mosque, to a grocery store, to a tax preparation center. The key feature is "everything is owned by a Somali and all business is conducted in Somali." English is not necessary.

---

[14] Field research done for unpublished doctoral dissertation by Enoch Wan, "The Dynamics of Ethnicity: A Case Study on the Immigrant Community of N.Y. Chinatown." State University of New York at Stony Brook.

Historically in the U.S., ethnic enclaves were seen as transition zones. Immigrants would arrive and find housing and work within the enclave at first, but gradually learn English and job skills that allowed them to transition out of the enclave. In time, Irish immigrants became Irish-Americans, and then simply Americans. Such a model seems to have been most common among European enclaves. However, the story is often different for other immigrants. The enclave is seen as a destination rather than a transition period (Portes and Bach 1985). This is particularly true of the Cuban enclave in Miami that Portes has studied for many years. Thriving enclaves like this require two components to last long term. The first is the enclave needs to have been started by a first stream of immigrants with money and business sense to get an ethnic economy going. Secondly, the enclave needs a continual stream of new immigrants that provide the workforce to keep the economy going. These two features are only found in a few long-term enclave environments today – for example Little Havana in Miami and the Chinatowns in New York City. Once immigration ceases, it isn't long before the enclave dies out as has been the case with numerous Vietnamese enclaves around the U.S.

Enclaves are not always the rosy environment as some may depict. In the Fuzhounese enclaves in NYC Chinatowns, researchers have discovered a vast human smuggling ring. Chinese smugglers and mafia ensure safe passage for illegal Chinese immigrants from China to NYC. In return, the immigrants must pay a $50,000 transportation debt and remain at the mercy of business owners, muck like an indentured servant, for years. These owners drastically exploit their own people in order to keep their businesses going. Immigrants do not find high paying jobs, but are often relegated to work under the table at home sewing material for the garment industry, or in many West Coast enclaves, assembling electronic circuit boards for well under minimum wage and at great risk to personal health due to the chemicals and glues involved in the process. These secret services allow companies to keep labor costs to a minimum and company profits high (Ong 2003). Compliance is enforced via threats, torture, rape, and kidnapping. Researchers conclude that many enclaves provide easy entrance into the U.S., but seriously question any long-term benefits of such a system.

A key characteristic of enclaves is high cultural pressure for new immigrants to retain their ethnic identity. Enclaves are as close as you can get to plucking a village out of one country and setting it down in the middle of a city in another country. Large enclaves use cultural pressure, much like the city would use police and government, to enforce cultural norms and dissuade people from changing, accepting new religions, and so on. There is little assimilation in the enclave, the heart language or native tongue is common, and little English is necessary. Enclaves produce a strong insider/outsider mentality and territoriality due to heavy cultural pressure to retain ethnic values. For this reason, church planting by outsiders in an enclave is particularly challenging.

Cultural Threads

This metaphor of cultural threads came to my mind as I researched immigrant in London, England. For a variety of reasons, immigrants in London are dispersed and enclaves do not readily form. I walked down the street and saw people from so many different cultural backgrounds, often living in the same flat together. As I talked with them, I realized that even though they lived geographically distant from other members of their ethnic group, it was like they had their finger on an invisible thread that linked them to their people. From a distance, the threads looks like they were entangled in a massive ball of yarn, but up close, the connections were there.

Generally, the idea of community is rooted in a place, as in geographic nearness. However, in a globalized and urbanized world, community is really about a shared collective cultural consciousness (Amit 2002). Immigrants share a cultural identity that leads to the idea of community even though they may live miles apart from each other. The technical term for this phenomenon is heterolocalism – a connected dispersion. Immigrants following this pattern of assimilation first seek out informal networks where they can feel connected, determine their social status in the new environment, and begin their new life. Later, they find or create more formal organizations that serve as a cultural unifier and reinforce for their ethnic group.

The organizational means that link the ethnic group together in the community may be churches, temples, mosques, community centers, business associations, bars, ethnic grocery stores, ethnic malls, English as a Second Language centers, annual cultural festivals, and so on. For example, in Dallas, Texas, there are no real ethnic enclaves. Instead, immigrants attain community through this cultural threads model. South Asian Indians have bought old strip malls that now contain restaurants, grocery and clothing stores, travel agencies, and Bollywood theatres. These centers of cultural exchange provide a place for migrant-community affirming events (Levitt 2000). These places and gatherings reinforce the cultural identity of the ethnic group in the face of segregated everyday life which pulls the individual toward the mainstream culture. In the case of the Indian immigrant, attending a festival helps the person feel more "Indian" and affirm his place as an Indian in American society and gives him a right to be different.

An additional "place" that needs to be taken into account is the virtual realm. Ethnic groups produce websites, chatrooms, and discussion boards where they can connect, find potential spouses, stay abreast of the latest news from their country, and provide advice for incoming immigrants on where to live and work. One example is the Ek Nazar (www.eknazar.com) website and database for the Indian community in Dallas. This website contains not only information but has become an economy in itself. Indian travel agencies use the site to market to Indians travelling back to India for vacation or a permanent move. The site is testing the market with Indians living in other cities like Atlanta, Houston, Detroit, and San Francisco.

Interestingly, the general population is often not aware that there is any connection between their Indian neighbor in the suburbs and the thousands of other Indians in the city. Up to 10,000 Indians live in Louisville, KY but they are largely invisible due to their disbursement. Church planters can sometimes mistakenly assume that immigrants in a diverse environment lose their individual ethnic identity and take on general characteristics of "Americanism" in a multicultural neighborhood. Such was the thinking of missionaries I worked with in London who were using a general church planting strategy of gathering ethnically diverse immigrants for an ESL club and then attempting to launch Bible studies out of the club. Research revealed that the majority of immigrants in London were connected via this cultural thread and had much less in common with other ethnic groups than could be seen on the surface.

In summary, the cultural thread model of assimilation consists of creating community through establishing habitual places of contact, congregation, worship, and ethnic identity confirmation and reinforcement. Groups most likely to assimilate via this model are those with high levels of human capital that have no need to group into an enclave and have the means to choose where they want to live and work in their destination city. They may live geographically dispersed, but remain connected through their cultural thread.

Urban Tribe

I sat in the community room of an apartment complex dominated by newly arrived refugees. I told the story of God calling Abraham to leave Ur and follow Him as Nepali Hindus, Iraqi Muslims, loosely Catholic Haitians, and a smattering of others listened in. We had been meeting every Tuesday night for several weeks, using the Bible stories as the basis for a conversational English class. It seemed that these quite diverse refugees were willing to set aside their cultural differences in order to unite as refugees in need of English skills.

The urban tribe model of assimilation is almost a model of its own, rather than at the end of the scale on levels of assimilation. The concept arose because diversity is one of the markers of an urban area. The late anthropologist and missionary Paul Hiebert observed that "as societies grow larger, they attract different kinds of people who form their own cultural communities" (Hiebert 1995: 267). In small villages, everyone knows everyone else but the city is far too large for such intimate interaction. Hiebert believed that immigrants prefer to relate closely to people in their own groups and view the majority of people they come in contact with as strangers.

Hiebert follows a classic model of anthropology that studies ethnic groups in relative isolation, almost as a silo unto themselves, even in a diaspora context. However, modern anthropologists believe people groups can no longer be studied in isolation, especially in the city. Culture in general is increasingly marked by hybridity. People are transnational, moving back and forth from immigration setting to home country, and begin to share components of many cultures (Rynkiewich 2011). Globalization and technology expose people to other cultures, particularly the West, at a pace never before seen in history. Whereas anthropologists used to study a tribe, they need to increasingly study "the tribe," especially in the city. The urban tribe concept defines a group of diverse individuals that share a common affinity of some kind that is so strong that it transcends their individual cultural identities. In some cases, the urban tribe is centered on shared affinity for a trade language or ethnic marker, while others are based on interest in sports, business, school, and a host of other markers.

What does all this have to do with ethnic church planting? Essentially, does our standard people group theory hold up in an immigrant, urban setting? Chris Clayman of Global Gates in New York City wrote the following in an email:

> Migration reshapes people group boundaries. Even in their home countries this takes place with urbanization, and many immigrants to NYC came from urban areas that are not considered "their ethnic homeland." So, we have many immigrants here that have been through, or are going through, two or more filtering processes in regards to their ethnic identity. Many of these [people] start having a much broader sense of their people group identity as a result.[15]

Clayman appears to be describing a scenario where people are moving "up" a level in their cultural identity. An example of the urban tribe concept follows: In Nigeria a Yoruba tribesman sees himself as distinct and very different from a Housa, though they may live in proximity to each other in the same country. They speak different languages, generally adhere to different religions (Yoruba are generally Christian, and Housa Muslim), and often war against each other. After immigrating to a city like NYC, however, the two peoples may drop their identity as Yoruba and Housa and simply think of themselves as "Nigerians" or even West Africans. They now speak their trade language or English rather than their tribal language and work together to survive in the U.S. as immigrants.

The implications of this thinking and the urban tribe in general inform the level of specificity and contextualization a church planter would need to reach people groups in an urban diaspora context. Does one need to learn Yoruba or Housa, or would English suffice? Can a Yoruba and Housa – traditional enemies – be expected to attend the same ESL class together or even an

---

15This email was cited in an article by Troy Bush, "Urbanizing Panta ta Ethne" in Journal of Evangelism and Missions (Vol. 12, Spring 2013): 12.

exploratory Bible study together in NYC? The urban tribe phenomenon is relatively new in missiology circles. More research certainly needs to be done to gauge how strong the affinity identity really is.

Several questions need to be asked when someone feels they are encountering an urban tribe. First, is the tribe mentality functioning at the worldview level or the social level? Worldview answers the deepest questions of life and meaning like who is God, how do we relate to him/her/it, where did we come from, how do we relate to each other, what causes sickness, how is it cured, and other questions about the afterlife. It may be possible that people composing an urban tribe are only making surface level accommodation to get along. They realize if they too strongly and publically express their worldview and religious beliefs, friction can result. So they go along to get along. Are Yorubas really moving "up" a people group level or are they adapting some kind of functional surface level cultural accommodation?

For example, there are two churches, one in Dallas and the other in Louisville which were planted to be intentionally multi-ethnic. At first, each church attracted people from a variety of ethnic groups. The Louisville church translated sermons from English into Nepali, Arabic, and Swahili. Each church had a unified Sunday gathering and then used weekly small group meetings in a mono-linguistic setting for discipleship. Over time in both churches, more and more immigrants arrived. Eventually, the individual ethnic groups approached the church and asked if they could begin meeting on their own so they could worship in their own language and in their own cultural style. It seems that the urban tribe, with the unifying affinity of "Christian immigrant" only held up at the functional level. Once enough people from the individual ethnic groups arrived, the groups felt more comfortable worshipping in a mono-ethnic context.

A common church planting strategy for reaching internationals and immigrants is to begin with an ESL class to meet functional needs of immigrants. The idea is to use the class to gather people together and then bridge to a Bible study and eventually a church plant. However, this strategy does not always work out this way. Immigrants, again, may only be coming together to gain the English skills they need to survive. Once the ESL class begins addressing worldview issues with a Bible study, the urban tribe falls apart. Why? Immigrants are willing to set aside their individual ethnic and cultural identities to gain survival skills. But it is my theory that once their worldview is questioned, their ethnic identity rises to the surface once again. Such was the case in London were I conducted ethnographic research for a mission agency. Immigrants from a host of Latin American countries and a handful of other people groups would gather for ESL. On the surface they seemed to be an urban tribe. They lived together in apartments and sometimes travelled around the city together. But once missionaries attempted to use the English club to launch a Bible study, the tribe disappeared. That diverse people lived together could be explained as a result of the narrow visa and housing problems immigrants have to deal with in London. The government made it difficult for an immigrant to live wherever he wanted. Often, he had to take the first opening he could find, regardless of the geographic location or current ethnic makeup of the housemates.

The urban tribe phenomenon is not entirely a myth, however. I feel that it is in operation on many college campuses. The reason is college students are often most open to trying new things. After all, international students are at the top of their peers and have left their country to study elsewhere. As individuals in a foreign environment, it is comforting for them to relate to others in the same situation. International students like to spend time with other international students. They understand each other's struggles. Additionally, as some research has shown, early stages of immigration may also produce the urban tribe for the same reasons. So perhaps taking a broad affinity based urban tribe strategy for church planting could be an effective way to begin ministry with immigrants. But, if overtime as more immigrants arrive, church planters must be prepared to adjust their strategy accordingly. Chapter 9 will discuss church planting strategies contextualized to each of these three assimilation patterns.

Assimilation Analysis

I have reviewed three models of assimilation above: the ethnic enclave, the cultural thread, and the urban tribe. Each model contains certain characteristics based on immigrant background, forms of capital, and location in the city. Each model requires a varying level of assimilation, but to some degree, all require some form of spanning boundaries between ethnic peoples themselves and the host culture. Boundary spanning is the key for assimilation (Alba and Nee, 2003). Boundaries exist in relation to social factors like language, religion, and family structure. Two main distinctions can be made regarding boundaries – boundary crossing and boundary blurring.

Boundary crossing occurs when an individual moves from one group to another without any change in the boundary itself. This type of assimilation is most common with those who change their names, habits, speech, and behavior from the outgroup patterns to the ingroup or majority culture patterns. In some cases, boundary crossing may take multiple generations but is accelerated through intermarriage that produces offspring who look physically closer to the majority culture.

Boundary blurring, on the other hand, changes the character of the boundary itself. A primary example of boundary blurring happens in a marriage of two people with different religious affiliations. Research shows that in many of these instances, both religions are recognized and religious rituals are shared by the family. In this case, religious boundaries have not disappeared, nor have both parties committed to only practicing one religion.

Rather, the boundary is blurred as elements of both religions are practiced. Boundary blurring relies on stable, ongoing social relationships and close contact. In some cases, immigrants following the cultural thread model of assimilation may take on multiple religious identities that blur into cultural identity as well. For example, a Hindu from India may blur his religious identity in the "Christian" U.S. and also view himself as a Christian or even call himself a Christian Hindu.

In summary, it is difficult to predict how immigrants will assimilate or make blanket statements on assimilation. However, based on studies of assimilation, several general patterns surface related to the forms of capital the immigrant brings. Those with human capital tend to assimilate easier because their resources allow them greater freedom when finding employment and housing. These immigrants are most likely to follow the cultural thread model of assimilation and adhere to heterolocalism. These immigrants live spatially separate but are culturally connected much more than may first appear. Immigrants bringing social capital are more likely to group into enclaves because they are reliant on their social network to find work and a place to live. Their lack of English and education limit their job selection. In some cases, the enclave environment requires little assimilation because everything needed for life can be found in the enclave neighborhood. Finally, those immigrants that are highly mobile, both geographically and culturally, have been theorized to form a new group, the urban tribe, based on their affinity interests. These immigrants almost over assimilate and take on highly intensified characteristics of a sub-culture within the larger dominant culture.

Formation of Cultural Identity

Instead of thinking of cultural identity as an already accomplished fact, it is better to think of identity as a production and process that is never finished (Hall 2003: 234). This understanding is especially important in the diaspora and immigrant context where pressures of the multi-cultural nature of urban life constantly challenge understandings of identity and belonging. In the diaspora, immigrants form a culture of micro-identities in the midst of the larger mainstream culture. This sense of culture carries the idea of both becoming and being as the immigrant struggles to reconcile past, present, and future understandings of cultural identity. Families have a shared past but are adjusting and assimilating to a new culture in a new geographic location. A child asks his father, "Am I Indian or American?" and is given the answer that he is both. Talk about an identity crisis!

Cycle of Cultural Identity

The path of immigration, choices made regarding level of assimilation, and then an understanding and expression of cultural identity is a difficult process. Identity is not static but moves along a spectrum, and moves at different paces for different people. A common scenario plays out with four steps on the path to assimilation and cultural identity. First, the immigrant leaves the home country because of all that is wrong there – the political corruption, poverty, the war, ect. Second, the immigrant embraces the new country for all of its idealism. The myth of the American Dream draws people to the U.S. more than any country in the world. Immigrants come with hopes of becoming wealthy. Third, life does not go as the immigrant desires. He becomes disillusioned with the U.S. and begins to look back at the good of the old ways from the home country. Fourth, the immigrant must decide either to live a balance of the old identity coupled with the new, abandon the old ways, or embrace and intensify the old ways but now in an idealized way.

The dominant culture of the U.S. plays a role in immigrant identity as well. In essence, racial and ethnic prejudice can force minority groups to gather together and intensify their ethnic identity. Blacks become "more black" in order to distance themselves from white mainstream America. Indians become "more Indian" for the same reason. Depending on where the immigrant and his immediate community are on the scale of assimilation, the ethnic identity may be very strong, to the point of rejecting identification as an American who happens to be ethnically Indian.

There are three general stages in an immigrant's understanding of ethnic identity (Radhakrishnan 2003). First, in order to be successful in the U.S., immigrants are sometimes forced to hide their distinct ethnic identity and assimilate. Second, after immigrants become more secure financially and socially, they look for a reaffirmation of their ethnic identity. This stage is described above in the section on cultural threads where immigrants assert their "right to be different." Third, many immigrants begin using a hyphenated integration of ethnic identity with U.S. national identity. These immigrants, by their very assimilation and citizenship in the U.S., are forced to make a decision: Are they, in the case above, Indian-Americans or are they Americans who happen to be Indian by ethnicity? The former retains a bit of ethnic pride and identity. The latter relegates ethnicity to secondary status behind new found American nationality.

Public-Private Identities

Often, dynamics of identity vary in public and private life as well. In a city, no group can live totally as it wishes. Publically, immigrants must play the role assigned to them by their employer and follow the general cultural norms or risk constant friction. Privately, people can be themselves. This behavior is similar to what linguists describe as code switching, the concept that individuals will speak one language or dialect in some instances but shift to another language or dialect when it is more appropriate given the social setting. Immigrant identity requires a type of cultural code switching that occurs between public and private life.

If church planters only encounter immigrants in the public sphere, they can be misled into believing immigrants have assimilated more than they really have. I feel this could be the case in many instances were church planters feel like they are dealing with an urban tribe. Privately, those same immigrants may express their identity very differently than they would in public. At home, they speak their native language and burn incense at the family altar. These scenarios underscore the importance of knowing people holistically, in both their public and their private lives.

Summary

This chapter has shown that assimilation strategy is a key factor in immigrant identity and plays out in three major scenarios in the city – ethnic enclaves, cultural threads or hetero-localism, and the urban tribe. The construction of ethnic identity is a complex issue, particularly in the urban diaspora setting. Immigrants struggle with who they are publically and privately and often change their own expression of who they are as they interact with others and adjust to life in a new environment. Church planters must beware of surface level functional assimilation as a means of survival without underlying worldview change. Furthermore, this transitioning identity should cause us to rethink our understandings of people groups in diaspora settings. Immigrants are not the same people, so to speak, as they were back home. The city pulls and pushes its residents and gradually reshapes the identity of immigrants. However, markers of diversity remain as assimilation is not an one-way endeavor. Immigrants contribute to the culture of the city just as they are shaped by it. Understanding this complexity and diversity is a beautiful but difficult reality, and one that is at the leading edge of diaspora missiology.

CHAPTER 6

IDENTIFYING AND UNDERSTANDING ETHNIC GROUPS IN THE CITY

Introduction

This chapter draws on and applies the findings presented in previous chapters. While certain patterns are predicable regarding assimilation, cultural identity, and orality preference, church planters need the tools to conduct their own research on their people in order to understand key dynamics in their own city. The first part of this chapter details how to identify a people group or groups in a complex urban environment. The second section focuses on a discussion of theory building that can give the church planter insight into the specific beliefs, identity, and needs of the target people to produce a contextualized ministry approach.

Conducting Ethnographic Research

The first step to reaching ethnic groups in the city is finding representatives from that people group and learning as much as one can about them. This kind of cultural research is generally referred to as ethnographic research. An ethnography is simply an in depth description of a people. Ethnographic research is not overly difficult and can be exciting and insightful. It is both an art and a science. It is a science in the sense that ethnography is driven by standardized research methods, careful note taking, and analysis of gathered data that is not haphazard. On the other hand, it's an art because the laboratory of the researcher is not sterile, controlled, and artificial. Ethnographic research takes place in the midst of real everyday human interaction and not in a created environment. The goal of the researcher is to see the world through the eyes of the culture under study. What better way to understand a people than to live life with them, see their struggles, feel their pain, and celebrate their culture?

In order to most effectively communicate the gospel and plant churches that do not look foreign in the context, the church planter must understand how the target people view life. To most people, perception is reality, even if this perception is not technically accurate. For example, when researching in one neighborhood in New York City I would ask people of different ethnic groups, "Who do you think is responsible for most of the crime in this neighborhood?" as one means to try and understand how people viewed and related to each other. I received strikingly different answers from each ethnic group. Of course, none of them thought their own group was responsible for crime and their perception of which group was "bad" had a dramatic impact on what kind of interaction they had with each other. If the Haitians perceived the Bengalis were responsible for the crime, it made no difference that I could show them a police report that revealed otherwise. To the Haitians, their perception that the Bengalis were thieves *was reality* to them, even though they were technically wrong. Ethnographic research helps the church planter learn all those perceptions that impact who might feel comfortable gathering together for Bible storying groups or other evangelistic events. Research will help explain not only *who is* there, but of equal importance, *who is not* and there and why.

Ethnographic research is both a process and an outcome. As a process, the researcher is able to become a participant observer, learning the culture from an insider's perspective. This insider's approach allows for exploration of culture and worldview issues and often raises many new questions that need to be answered. Additionally, participant observation allows for the building of deep relationships during the research process. Ethnographic research makes use of key informants, those cultural insiders who aid in the research process by providing the researcher credibility and insight into the community. Relationships are essential for effective church planting but even more so when the target population comes from a communal, relational culture like many of the immigrant groups in the U.S. Along the way, the researcher will learn valuable vocabulary, idioms, habits, community gatekeepers and leaders, degree of people group networking and connectedness, and places of residence that will be essential for the church planting process in the future. The time given to the process of thorough ethnographic research is not wasted time and is essential for effective ministry.

Ethnographic research is also an outcome of the process. The end goal is a cultural portrait that paints as close to a native's view of the culture as possible. The document will describe daily life and contain names, places, and observations from religious and cultural events. Ethnographies also contain analysis and interpretation of behavior that is vital for a contextualized church. This research looks at culture below the surface, rather than merely describing observable details. Such reports are useful tools for creating a strategy for effective ministry. Additionally, write-ups are useful for training perspective workers and interns, and also for presenting in various churches and meetings for mobilization purposes.

Ethnographic research is typically built on three legs – bibliographic research, participant observation, and ethnographic interviewing. This three-pronged approach provides well rounded research that is reliable and insightful. An additional "leg" is demographic research which consults census data and is useful to determine physical locations of immigrants in the country, state, or city.

Bibliographic Research

First, conducting bibliographic research helps the church planter find what others have already learned about the people and gives a general orientation to the culture. One can search online for the Joshua Project, Caleb Project, IMB global research, Operation World, SIL's Ethnologue, Ethnopedia, and a host of other people groups databases to get an idea of the language, religion, and cultural values of the target people group. Additionally, a trip to the local university library can yield books and journal articles describing the culture of the people. Bibliographic research is helpful because it begins to familiarize the church planter with the culture and enhances the actual field research that will come later.

General books on cultural values are helpful as well. Anthropologists have identified what they call a cultural spectrum on which every culture falls. One of the most helpful works on this topic is Sherwood Lingenfelter's *Ministering Cross-Culturally* (Lingenfelter and Mayers 2003). The book begins with a user survey to identify the reader's own cultural values and preferences and then goes on to briefly describe each value – Time vs Event orientation, Holistic vs Dichotomistic judgment, Crisis vs Non-Crisis orientation, Task vs Person orientation, Ascribed vs Achieved Status, and Concealment vs Exposure of Vulnerability. Understanding each of these values will help the church planter avoid frustration and cultural misunderstandings that could result in unnecessary offense. It's a good idea to administer the survey to members of the target people as well, to learn about their values, but also because it provides a great entry into conversation about significant biblical and cultural issues and can be a bridge to sharing the gospel.

Demographic Research

Bibliographic research is only one piece of the ethnographic puzzle. People and cultures change over time so books written years ago may no longer reflect the current situation. Additionally, immigration changes people, so books on Yoruba culture in Nigeria may not accurately reflect the values of

Yoruba immigrants in Cincinnati, Ohio. This is where ground level field research is essential. But, in order to talk with people, the researcher needs to find out where they actually live! Demographic research is a means to pinpoint general locations of immigrants in the United States.

Research at the national level. It is helpful to begin this complex research process at the highest level. Such research can help the church planter save time by finding specific states, counties, and even zip codes where his people live. Every year the Department of Homeland Security is tasked to provide documentation for all people granted legal immigration, refugee, asylum, naturalization, and non-immigrant admission status. The document they produce is called the *Yearbook of Immigration Statistics* and breaks down immigration by the immigrants' country of last residence, country of birth, state of current residence, gender, age, marital status, occupation, and so on. These categories are helpful for narrowing the search for a target people. The document does not classify immigrants by people group so its usefulness is limited in some cases. However, a general estimate of particular peoples can be made by searching the demographic data re: their country of origin. Field level research is required to identify the people group and is explained later in this chapter. National level demographic research is useful to find large concentrations of immigrants from a particular country in various U.S. states or identify certain types of immigrants by category, such as university students.

Missions strategists in particular can use the national report for fund raising or mobilization efforts. For example, it is difficult for Americans to get a visa to enter Iran for missionary purposes but nearly 20,000 Iranians legally immigrated to the U.S. last year so efforts can be launched to reach them here. The national report is a good place to begin because a vast amount of information is located in one place. The report narrows the search for a particular people to a particular state or type of immigrant and further research can be done at lower levels to focus the search even more.

Research at the state level. Individual states do not all keep a high level of statistical information on immigrants. I worked with immigrants in Kentucky for several years and found that Kentucky maintains no accessible statewide database. I called several departments in the capital city trying to obtain a breakdown of immigration by county or city. My inquiries resulted in no further information. Happily, not all states follow Kentucky's unhelpful model. There is a refugee database available that lists admissions by every state in the U.S. and includes a contact phone number to get more detailed information.[16] These offices are usually connected with local level governments, social services, and ministries that can provide much more detailed information about internationals in a specific city. In addition to the refugee database, many state government offices keep a record of immigration

---

[16]http://www.acf.hhs.gov/programs/orr/data/state_profiles.htm

statistics and can offer help to the researcher in locating specific peoples in the city or county of choice.

Research at the city level. Smaller cities may not keep immigration statistics at all but this does not mean one cannot find valuable local information about ethnic groups in the city. A good place to begin at the local level is to do an internet search or scan the phonebook for Catholic Charity Services, English as a Second Language centers, refugee centers, and neighborhood ethnic business associations. The city of Louisville even has a government webpage specifically for internationals living in the city. From this page, one can find information about ESL classes, translation services, and social services all designed to meet the needs of immigrants to Louisville. A phone call or visit to any one of these organizations will likely yield contact information and provide practical ways to meet internationals. Louisville also has an organization called Kentucky Refugee Ministries that provides many services to refugees including helping them find housing, jobs, learn English, and provides money to help with the transition to the U.S. Finally, local census offices can be of great help. Certain cities have planning commissions that organize census data collection. A visit to their office may yield detailed information for specific neighborhoods or boroughs in the city. Since many cities already have services in place designed to find and help immigrants, the researcher need not perform redundant research when he or she can take advantage of work that has already been done.

Additionally, The North American Mission Board has compiled a website devoted to listing statistics and information on as many people groups in North America as possible.[17] This website allows the researcher to view statistics for every state and Canadian province. All nationalities, languages spoken, and ancestries found in the state are listed. By registering and obtaining special login information, the researcher is able to further find a breakdown of specific people groups in each major city within the state. A profile is provided of each people group. These profiles are user entered so some cities have more detailed information than others. In Louisville, for example, I can find detailed information about the Bosnian population. The page lists their heart language, primary religion, population, zip codes where they live, and paragraphs describing their daily life in Louisville, needs, beliefs, gospel barriers, current efforts to reach them, and prayer guides. As noted, most of this information is user entered and there is a need for church planters to continually update the site as new information is discovered. Information of this level of detail can only be found through conducting personal field research.

---

[17]See "People Groups", http://www.peoplegroups.info/

Conducting Field Research

Reports and statistics are helpful for ascertaining demographic information and the general location of ethnic peoples in a city but at some point, fieldwork needs to be done. In some large cities, it can be difficult to physically locate someone from the target people, even though the census and demographic research notes they are there, somewhere.

Locating specific members of the target people group. Chapter 5 revealed that immigrants and refugees often congregate in apartment complexes in the city, many of which are part of a government housing program designed to help internationals transition into the U.S. There are multiple complexes in Louisville that are connected with Kentucky Refugee Ministries, a local social service organization, and house large numbers of ethnic peoples. Finding a contact person in one of the apartment complexes will often lead the researcher to many more people within the group. A listing of apartments housing immigrants and refugees may be obtained through a visit to the local immigrant social services facility.

Immigrants following the cultural threads or urban tribe model of assimilation may not live together in the same apartment complex. However, many large cities have international festivals every year and these events are excellent places to meet scores of internationals. Ethnic communities usually have booths set up to showcase their food and culture. Those hosting the booths are often excellent resources for introducing the researcher to the culture. Appointments can be made for the researcher to visit homes or places of worship of the host and these appointments can result in many opportunities for ministry.

Another place to meet internationals is an ethnic grocery store. One can simply open the phone book and look for ethnic food stores and make a visit. Cities have many such stores and the owners and employees are often friendly and enjoy a visit from an American. Genuine interest in the food can lead to good conversation with the workers. A good idea is to invite an employee to your house in order to learn how to cook a favorite dish from their country of origin.

Cities are home to colleges and universities. These schools have various international clubs and cultural events that draw many ethnic peoples. A researcher may scan the website of a school in town and find contact information for someone leading one of the international clubs. Additionally, many schools have some kind of program designed to connect internationals with Americans for language and cultural instruction. Many colleges also have a TESOL (teaching English to speakers of other languages) or ESL (English and a second language) program for students who are accepted on a provisional basis, that they might learn enough English to enroll in an academic program. Such language programs are often looking for volunteers from the community to befriend internationals and help them with their English. Additionally, colleges often have campus ministries that draw international students and are great places to meet people.

Apartment complexes, international festivals, ethnic grocery stores, and college campuses are all good places to meet internationals. Immigrants are often highly connected with others from their ethnic group so meetings can lead to many more contacts. Taking the time to have a good conversation begins to build the relationship and many internationals are open to having American friends. The researcher should not be afraid to be bold in asking to visit the international at his house or inviting him to visit the researcher's house.

Once a neighborhood is located where pockets of immigrants live, the researcher then conducts "street ethnography" focused on likely congregation sites of the target population. Walking the area helps the researcher find shops, libraries, and parks where the target population frequent. In past personal research, I have found that there are people in every neighborhood who seem to know quite a bit about what goes on and can help me answer key questions and point me to more productive areas to find what I am looking for.

Key informants are needed, especially in the early stages of research. These informants are crucial to the success of research among hidden populations for two reasons. First, informants are insiders who can provide information about the locations, behaviors, suspicions, and necessary approaches to speaking with immigrants. Second, informants provide the researcher access and credibility in the community. Key informants were critical for my research of immigrants in London. Having a Portuguese speaking cultural insider clearly eased suspicion with those Brazilian immigrants I interviewed. The importance of language and trust was further emphasized as I interviewed an Afghani who spoke fluent English. I had with me a Pakistani informant who spoke English and Urdu. We were conducting the interview in English and good information was slow in coming. At one point, the Afghani said something to my informant in Urdu and from then on, the conversation was much more open and helpful. After leaving, I asked my informant what the Afghani asked him in Urdu. He said he had asked if we, as outsiders, were to be trusted. My informant assured him we were trustworthy. This interaction, and many like it, showed me the value of not only a key informant, but one who speaks the local language as well.

Another approach to locate and build relationships with ethnic peoples is to recruit members of the population to a specific geographic location in the neighborhood. One idea is to use a van that functions as a mobile research station. Researchers can drive a clearly marked van around the neighborhood and pass out needed items like warm clothes, maps, bus tickets, and information about events that can help immigrants. Over time, people become familiar with the presence of the van and recruitment can increase. A second recruitment method, perhaps after beginning with a mobile van, is to rent a storefront shop and use it as a field station for research. Such a practice places the researcher in a known location in the neighborhood long term and builds familiarity and rapport. These temporary field stations can be places were immigrants can stop by for coffee, tea, snacks, and information or classes for English as a Second Language, practice driving cars and preparing for a licensure examination, citizenship preparation classes, or other research identified needs in the community. Providing these practical helps increases the likelihood of immigrants coming to the research station where the researcher can then learn about the community.

Finally, the researcher should conduct an ethnographic mapping project of the community. This map should list the geographic disbursement of the target people, their places of employment, highly frequented shops and restaurants, places of worship, and locations of key informants. Such mapping helps the researcher identity geographic boundaries of the target people and can be useful to determine the most strategic locations to start churches. Modern technology such as smart phones and computer tablets make mapping an easy process. For example, one can download the app *FieldNotes*. This app allows the researcher to mark the global position (GPS) of the site, record field notes audibly and textually, take a picture of the interviewee or site location, and record a video of the interview or location. This data can be saved in a variety of formats compatible with geographic information systems programs like Google maps and Google Earth. The researcher can export the data to these web programs and generate a map of all data points recorded with the *FieldNotes* app. Data can then be sorted according to any number of categories determined by the researcher such as language family, religious affiliation, informant, and various needs like ESL class, driving school, or citizenship test preparation.

Participant observation. Once you hav found areas of the city where your target people live, it is time to walk the streets and get to know them. Participant observation is a research method that helps you "walk a mile in their shoes" so to speak. This kind of research reminds me of Sherlock Holmes, who was the master of observation. Holmes could walk into a room and "see" things that others missed and it was often in the details that he pieced clues together that could solve the mystery. We as researchers are after those same details and participant observation is a skill that, thankfully, can be honed with experience.

The best way to begin is to find or bring along someone from the group you want to learn more about. These individuals can make all the difference in accessing sites and people you need to talk to. I remember walking the infamous Cabrini Green projects in Chicago and had along a woman who grew up there and had the respect of many of the residents. We were able to go into projects and houses that the gang leaders would have otherwise certainly barred us from entering. This woman gave us as outsiders credibility that she herself had built over the years. In some cases, locals are happy to share their expertise with you and will gladly introduce you to important people and places in the community.

There are three levels of participation that should be considered, depending on the situation and ethical concerns involved. First is non-participant observation. Some cultural situations are not appropriate for outsiders to participate in. For example, you may be walking the streets and witness a drug deal going down. Observing this situation is beneficial to get an idea of the local economy, but as a church planter, you obviously would not participate in the deal. In a different situation, one of my friends had been building a relationship with the Sudanese Dinka population in Louisville and they invited him to observe a wedding dowry negotiation. Not being Dinka, he could not actually play a role in the negotiation, but what a wonderful and fascinating opportunity to learn about how Dinka handle this important part of their culture in a diaspora context.

A more involved level is partial participation. Here, the researcher is able to join in the activity to a limited degree, but will not play a central role. For example, I was in New York City and saw a group of Bengali boys playing cricket in a park. I had no experience with cricket and didn't know the rules, nor was I on the cricket team the boys were, but they let me join in for a few rounds. The opportunity allowed me to ask a few questions about the role of cricket in their culture and learn ways Bengali boys socialize in NYC. My limited participation was fun and informative, but I was not playing a key role in the community.

Full participation is when the researcher has an essential and integral part of the cultural process. A local church planter may be able to have an official seat at a local ethnic business association and even vote on issues. This level of participation is ideal in many ways, foremost because the researcher is fully immersed in the community – his or her concerns and struggles are the same as the target people. Often, full participation is only possible after several months or years of building relationships and gaining the right to speak into the culture and community as an insider.

Whatever the level of participation, the researcher should be doing more than simply joining in. It is helpful to make notes and describe what is happening in detail, who is there, what role does each person seem to have, how are people dressed, who interacts with whom, what are the non-verbal gestures, what items are on the wall, in the car, etc. These observations give insight into culture. I have a friend in Argentina who kept noticing red ribbons tied onto car antennas, bikes, and baby strollers. At first, he thought nothing of it, but eventually began to notice that these ribbons were everywhere. He finally asked someone what they meant and found out that people used them to ward off the evil eye. People believed that if someone looked on your car or baby with jealously, the spirits could bring sickness or bad luck to you. The ribbon scared away the spirits and took the power away from the evil eye.

Participant observation builds relationships with people in the community and helps them begin to feel more comfortable with you. It also should raise many questions about the culture that can be answered through interviewing people in the community. As you grow in observation skills, you will notice the details that are key to understanding the culture. Always be on the lookout. I was walking through a community garden with Nepali friends once and noticed ribbons and odd symbols near some of the plots. My observation led to asking questions about their meaning. I learned a little about the spiritual beliefs of the people and this helped me understand important issues to address with the Bible as we worked through Bible storying with the community. Observation should always lead to questions that are closely informed by aspects of the culture. In some ways, interviewing people is second nature, but to get the most out of the process, there are a number of issues to consider.

Ethnographic interviewing. It is very important to understand people's experiences from their point of view. One of the best ways to accomplish this task is by getting out and talking to people. Ethnographic interviewing provides a window into people's life experiences, perceptions of the neighborhood, and can even help the researcher begin to understand important local historical events in which you didn't actually participate but have a lasting impact on community interaction. Interviewing is a research tool, just like a library, and builds on skills you already have. It is a conversation, but one where the goal is to intentionally learn about people's thoughts, feelings, and experiences. Unlike a casual conversation, here the researcher asks a limited number of questions and encourages the interviewee to provide detail and depth on their experiences. In this way, the researcher can let the research build a theory about what is going on in the area and not import foreign explanations.

The researcher is the most important tool in ethnographic interviewing and must keep in mind several considerations for effective interviews. 1) Be flexible and realize that every interview is likely to be different, even if you ask the same types of questions. People have different experiences and perspectives so they may respond in a variety of ways to the same situation. 2) Be sure to listen first and then follow up as information unfolds. It is easy to begin to fill in the blanks after you have talked with a number of people, but you never know when you have met someone that can provide a key insight that you will miss if you talk too much and make assumptions. 3) Look for detail and ask follow up questions to further draw out detail. One of my favorite follow up questions is "Why do you think that is?" Often, the *why* is more important than the *what*. 4) Attempt to appear relaxed. Interviewing strangers can be intimidating. Having a local friend along is helpful. People are likely to be suspicious of you if they don't know you. Are you with the government or immigration services? They may question your intentions for getting information out of them.

The interviewee is a partner in the research, not the object of the research. They are the experts on their own people and community and you as the researcher are the learner. They can open doors in the community that you cannot. It is usually helpful to let people know what you are researching and why. For example, when I was researching Inuit culture in Iqaluit, Nunavut, Canada, people were regularly suspicious of me and commented Iqaluit was "crawling with anthropologists" who were out to use them for their own research and dissertations and would leave when they were done, without a care for the Inuit themselves. I tried to explain that our research purposes were different. I explained that we wanted to know a bit of the history, culture, and relations of the Inuit because we hoped to send people to plant churches in the community. We told them we believed the gospel was the only means of hope in a difficult society with some of the highest suicide rates in the world and increasing problems with drugs and alcohol. We said so because the Inuit are created by a loving God we want to see them restored to relationship with Him. Clearly explaining why we were there and what we hoped to do with the research helped reduce suspicion that otherwise naturally existed.

It is a good idea to interview a wide variety of people in the community from different age brackets as well. Find people in local shops, on their porches, bus stops, community centers, libraries, and places of worship. I like to talk with any police officers as well so I can get their opinion of the community dynamics. Make a habit of asking each person if they know someone else you should talk with or some place you should visit. It is even better if they can introduce you to those people and places to gain instant credibility. Try to find the cultural gatekeepers if possible – those people who are respected and can speak accurately for the culture. Usually, gatekeepers are easy to find by just asking people who are the most helpful people to talk with. Help people understand that you want to learn from them because they know the area better than you. Try to quickly learn local slang words when referring to places, especially. Avoid words like ethnographic research, people groups, ect. Experiment with ways to introduce yourself and your purposes and see which works best in that given location.

It is a good idea to have a multi-ethnic team with you if possible. Sometimes it helps for a non-white to talk to a non-white. They may have shared experiences as minorities or immigrants and can quickly build rapport. Other times, it can be helpful for a white to talk with a non-white. You might ask, "How do you think white people view your people in this community?" Being white yourself means you may be able to do something about the problem. Another benefit of researching with a team is there is almost always a mixture of extroverts and introverts. Extroverts are good at beginning initial conversation while introverts might be able to follow up with additional questions.

In some situations, note taking is okay during the interview but it is usually best to step aside after the conversation and take notes. Always take notes right away or else it is too easy to forget important details. Recall the conversation with your team and write notes in a small notebook or in your *Field Notes* phone or tablet app. With *Field Notes* you should also record the GPS location of the interview and take a picture of the area and list the address. Later, you can upload all of the GPS points to Google maps and the interview notes and pictures will stay with the file.

Ethnographic research is crucial for understanding the cultural dynamics of the people you want to reach with the gospel. Combining book research, participant observation, and ethnographic interviewing provides the most accurate picture of the community. The goal is to identify the cultural identity, expression, and worldview of the people in order to contextualize the church in the community. Now that this section has covered the basics of the research process, we will explore worldview and provide a framework for learning the worldview of your people.

Identifying Cultural Identity of Immigrants

Understanding and expressing cultural identity is a complex and often fluid process. In general, worldview is the driving factor in expression of culture, though closely related cultures often share the same worldview. It is important to understand the nuances of worldview, as it is expressed through cultural production and identity in an immigrant setting. Orality preference also factors in with regards to expression of cultural identity because core worldview beliefs are often reinforced and acted out through oral communication methods like stories, rituals, and dramas. Therefore, to gain a full picture of cultural identity in a diaspora setting, one must understand both worldview and orality preference.

Worldview Identification

It is important to understand as best as possible how the people identify themselves and express their culture in their diaspora setting. It is not enough to simply know someone as a "Muslim" or "Hindu." What matters is how that religious identity plays out in their public and private life, along with how much of their home culture continues to shape their identity. To help with this process, we have created a short worldview identification workbook included in Appendix 1, designed to be used in your community. The workbook is explained in detail here with the intention being for the researcher to grasp the basics now and then copy and print the appendix workbook to take into the community when conducting research.

A short survey can begin the process, which in its entirety, often takes several months to compile a credible understanding of the people group. The

CHAPTER 7

KEY ISSUES FOR EFFECTIVE URBAN, ETHNIC MINISTRY

Introduction

Urban ministry is very complex and each situation carries its own contextual issues, hence the importance of the preceding section focusing on ethnographic research methods. Once an understanding of the target people is reached, the church planter can begin to move toward specific strategies for evangelism and church planting. Before an actual strategy is implemented, the church planter must consider five primary philosophical and practical matters that need to be settled. 1) Will you plant multi or mono-ethnic churches? 2) How will you prepare to minister to oral preference people and develop a proper storyset? 3) How will you implement critical contextualization in order to plant churches that are biblically faithful and culturally understandable? 4) How will you mobilize and train churches for the immense task of urban, ethnic church planting? 5) What are key means to raise up indigenous leadership from within the community so the church is not always tied to outside leadership?

Decide Whether to Plant a Multi- or Mono-ethnic Church

Chapter 5 showed that immigrants primarily follow three patterns for assimilation – the enclave community, the connected cultural thread, and the urban tribe model. Two of these assimilation theories describe communities that are multi-cultural to some degree. In some occasions, immigrants from different backgrounds are forced by the government or intentionally choose to gather in the same neighborhood or apartment complex in order to maintain relationships and ease the tensions of culture shock. Some church planters may view such an apartment complex as an easy place to begin a ministry to ethnic peoples. This convenience also brings several inherent challenges. For example, there were Nepalese, Iraqis, Haitians, Chinese, South Asian Indians, and several African peoples living in the complex in which I ministered. How does one do ministry in a context filled with drastic differences in language, culture, religion, and worldview? In situations like this one, church planters are faced with the decision of whether to plant a mono or multi ethnic church.

The first question to be settled is whether there is a biblical command that a church be mono or multi ethnic. Your theology should drive your missiology, not the other way around. Once the biblical issue is settled, a strategy can be implemented to reach the target population. Three passages come to mind as potential support for the essentiality of a multi-ethnic church: Galatians 3, Ephesians 2, and Revelation 5:9.

Galatians 3:28-29

One passage cited to support the mandate of a multi-ethnic church is Galatians 3:25-29, especially verse 28 which states that "There is neither Jew nor Greek, there is neither slave nor free, there is neither male nor female, for you are all one in Christ Jesus." A casual response connects "there is neither Jew nor Greek" to "we must plant a multi-ethnic church." The question is, what does this passage mean when it states that "you are all one in Christ Jesus?" Is this a mandate for multi-ethnic church or is Paul making the point that all have access as one people, humanity, to Jesus Christ? I believe the latter is what Paul is getting at. He just finished a discussion of the purpose of the law, which was a guardian for the Jews as the people of God. No one could access God apart from essentially becoming culturally "Jewish" and following the law. However, now that Christ has come, the law is no longer the guardian nor the means of accessing God. As many as have been baptized into Christ have put on Christ, by faith and apart from the law (Gal. 3:26), and people no longer need to become cultural Jews to gain access to God.

Furthermore, some who use this passage as a mandate for multi-ethnic church only address the "neither Jew nor Greek" phrase and neglect the two others that follow in verse 28. If Christ abolishes ethnic distinction so that there is only "one in Christ," does this also mean that slaves are no longer slaves when they accept the gospel, or that the distinction between male and female no longer exists? Of course not. Those distinctions remain, just as people are still ethnically Jewish or ethnically something else after becoming a Christian. The point of this passage is not to abolish those distinctions, but to point out that all have access to God through Jesus Christ and so in that sense, it makes no difference if one is Jew, Greek, slave, free, male, or female. The gospel is for everyone.

Ephesians 2:11-22

Here, Paul is speaking to the Gentiles stating that at one time they were separated from Christ, alienated from the commonwealth of Israel and strangers to the covenants of promise, having no hope and without God in the world. Now they have been brought near by the blood of Christ, who has made both Jew and Greek one by breaking down the dividing wall of hostility, which Paul refers to as the law, and Christ creates in himself one new man in the place of the two, so making peace. The question here is what is the hostility that is spoken of and what is the "one new man?" Is it hostility between Jew and Greek? This passage can be read to refer to hostility, not between Jews and Greeks, but between Greeks and God. Specifically, Christ has broken down the dividing wall (which Paul emphasizes is the law of commandments and ordinances in verse 15) in himself and made access through the cross to true peace with God for both Jews and Greeks. Primarily, this passage most clearly reads that there are not two paths to God, and specifically that the law and its corresponding Jewish cultural elements is no longer the path, which in the past had excluded the Gentiles. Christ has abolished the law and there is no longer a need for Gentiles to become "Jews" to access God because Christ himself is the peace and the way to God. There is not clear enough evidence from this passage to support the conclusion that a church *must* be multi-ethnic as DeYmaz claims (DeYmaz 2007: 29-30).

Furthermore, one must ask if this passage is referring to Gentiles pre or post-conversion. While Galatians as a whole is written to the church, Paul here seems to be referring to Gentiles in their pre-conversion state. He is reminding them that before Christ they were separated from God and cut off from the house of Israel. The multi-ethnic church debate often overlooks what Donald MacGavran was really getting at – that people tend to *come to Christ* by crossing as few cultural barriers as possible. Paul is not saying in Galatians that cultural distinctions disappear or are not important. What he is actually saying is that people *can keep their own ethnic distinctions and still come to Christ*. They do not need to adopt a new cultural identity before being able to become a Christian.

Revelation 5:9 and 7:9

In these two verses, Christ is praised for his worthiness to be slain so that a multitude from every tribe, tongue, nation, and people might be found in heaven worshiping God. Some might argue that because heaven will be multi-cultural, so must the church on earth. This is indeed a beautiful picture of worship but is it a mandate for multi-cultural church on earth? I have two issues with this line of reasoning. First, these verses are describing a future reality, and one that we do not have extensive information on. We just do not know if everyone in heaven will speak the same language and share the exact same culture. We do know that we will worship together, but exactly what that will look like is impossible to discern. The main point in these passages is that Jesus' blood is enough for all. Second, there are many other realities that will be so in heaven but are not attainable on earth. I think of those who believe we can be totally free of sin while still on earth, and that the atonement ensures that Christians should no longer suffer from sickness, poverty, or abuse. This thinking is called over realized eschatology. Just because these will be future realities for our glorified bodies does not mean we can expect to or must experience these realities now.

The Authors' Position

There is a vast amount of writing and debate on the homogeneous unit principle and multi-ethnic church planting. In light of space constraints, we will state where we stand on the issue. We fully believe the gospel breaks down barriers that are the result of sin. Racism is a sin and must never be promoted or tolerated in the church. However, there are many, many cultural and linguistic barriers that are not sinful. There is no such thing as a "culture free gospel" or a "culture free church." In every case, a choice has to be made as to what style of music to use, what style of preaching to use, and what language to do it all in. Believe it or not, the American style of standing up front behind a pulpit and delivering a lecture style sermon is culturally driven. In other cultures, the teaching authority sits. People may not all sit side by side facing the front. Preaching styles vary widely. Just visit an African-American church, a southern country church, or Tim Keller's church in New York City. Each has a distinct "style" of what preaching is that reflects a certain cultural understanding. I am trying to make the point that many proponents of multi-ethnic church think only of their preferred style and feel it is the most biblical when in fact it is just a reflection of their own culture.

Furthermore, I believe that God delights in the diversity He has allowed to flourish on the earth. God is magnified when people from a host of linguistic and ethnic backgrounds worship him. I love multi-ethnic church. It is a beautiful thing to worship with Christians from Haiti, Afghanistan, Nigeria, and Columbia all together. But, it is also a beautiful thing to witness Afghani refugees worshipping Jesus in Urdu in New York City. I believe that God has given us the freedom to examine the cultural context and plant a church that will reach the greatest number of people within a given ethnic group.

I like to ask church planters, "Is your goal to plant a multi-ethnic church or is it to reach as many as possible in this community?" For many, the goal is just to plant a multi-ethnic church. So long as even one person from each ethnic group is in attendance, the church has reached its goal. But what of the rest of the people from those ethnic groups? Research shows that it is typically the "fringers" in a society that are most likely to attend multi-ethnic church.

These are the 5-10% of people in a group that are least like the core of that group. Churches need to ask the question "who are we reaching" but an even more important question is "who are we *not* reaching and why?" Sometimes the goal of reaching the community is accomplished by planting a multi ethnic church, but other times a mono ethnic church will reach the greatest number within the target people. I believe that multi-ethnic churches can be strategic when they are used as a training center. They may draw the fringe ethnic population, but the church can raise up church planters from within that group and send them back to the core of their people to plant a mono-ethnic church in the group's heart language that is the most likely to reach those at the center of the culture that hold their ethnic identity the tightest.

Remember that this book primarily focuses on first generation immigrants who likely retain a strong preference for their heart language. The very nature of multi-ethnic church requires a choice for which language to worship in. Whatever language is chosen, someone is left out. Must we always require people to worship God in their second, third, or fourth language? What if they prefer to worship in their first language? Is this sinful? Many times, multi-ethnic churches reflect the character of the majority culture in the area and marginalize ethnic minorities. I have a friend who is church planting professor who happens to also be Hispanic. He likes to say, "Me, I'm a huge fan of multi-ethnic church. Let us have the service in my language, Spanish, and let everyone either learn it or listen to preaching through a translator." This statement is a poke at the majority of multi-ethnic churches that use English as their primary language and expect everyone to accommodate. Many of these churches do use translators, but it is very difficult for anyone to really feel connected to the church when they always hear everything through a translator. First generation ethnic ministry might require use of the immigrant's heart language so in these cases, a multi-ethnic church is just not a viable strategy. In light of my position, I want to introduce a number of questions that need to be dealt with when considering whether to plant a mono or multi ethnic church.

Challenges to Consider

The city is diverse; there is no doubt about that. While large cities like Chicago, New York, and San Francisco have distinct ethnic communities like Chinatown, Little Italy, and so on, many cities have no clear ethnically geographic boundaries. Cities like Louisville have sections of town where immigrants and refugees tend to live but many ethnic groups are represented in the same geographical area. Functionally, distinct people groups sometimes come together in the city to form an urban tribe community such as that described in Chapter 5. Refugees in parts of Louisville rally around their refugee status; they are all trying to find jobs, they attend the same ESL classes, they shop at the same grocery store, and they live in the same apartment complex. But do they have more in common with each other than with their individual ethnic identity? If so, it makes sense to plant a multi ethnic church since a new homogenous group has arisen – those sharing refugee status. Immigrants try to take advantage of their situation in order to find stability and jobs. If mixing with other ethnic groups allows a sense of stability, they might set aside their cultural distinctions based on current affiliations. However, if given the chance, would these people revert to their respective mono ethnic communities?

Some research indicates that multi ethnic communities that originally group around a common affinity will indeed revert to mono ethnic and mono linguistic communities once a sufficient number of their ethnic group arrives in the city. For example, historically, immigrants to Mumbai, India lived in ethnically diverse communities upon arrival. The northern part of the city was the industrial center and immigrants would cluster in neighborhoods within walking distance of the factories where they worked. At first, the immigrants had more in common with each other than they did with the ethnic villages they left. In fact, the caste system was not able to be enforced as strictly because of the ethnic diversity. In time, though, as more and more immigrants arrived, mono ethnic and mono linguistic communities formed around the factories and the caste system was again enforced.[19]

Similarly, Grant Lovejoy, International Mission Board orality expert, is finding that some multi ethnic churches experience splits once a critical mass of mono ethnic peoples arrive in town. Even church plants focused on East Africans as an urban tribe have split as a sufficient number of ethnic tribals arrive. The church service had been in Swahili, the trade language of Eastern Africa, but after the split, the individual mono ethnic churches worshipped in their home/heart language. These splits did not result out of anger or bitterness, just out of a preference for language. Such splits do not always occur but as multi ethnic church planting becomes more popular and the congregations are given enough time to gain a larger number of people from the same ethnic background, more mono ethnic groups are leaving the multi ethnic church context to form their own church.

An important question is whether the church planter will be prepared for such a split or not. Will he insist on a multi-ethnic church as the only true expression of gospel unity? Or will he allow the gospel to reach the largest number of people possible within each ethnic group? Certainly, any racism or discrimination that drives a church split is sinful and is not a legitimate reason to form a separate ethnic church. However, many of these reasons described are not racist and are not inherently sinful. Of course, it is a wonderful idea for

---

[19]Anthony Casey, "A Missiological Portrait of Bombay, India," http://culturnicity.files. wordpress.com/2011/04/bombayfinal.pdf (accessed September 3, 2013).

mono ethnic churches to gather together on occasion with other churches in the area and celebrate as the family of God.

These theological and practical questions must be settled on the front end of church planting in order to avoid unnecessary heartache later. The mono or multi ethnic church planting discussion leads to the next issue. Many immigrants and refugees come from primary or secondary oral cultures so church planters need to be prepared to minister accordingly. Chapter 4 described the oral worldview in depth and the section below will discuss the application of oral strategies for church planting in urban areas.

Utilizing Orality Strategies

Oral communicators are found in every cultural group in the world. If the source is correct, sixty to seventy percent of the world's population prefers a non-literate approach to learning (Claydon 2005: 3). In the recent past, many churches welcomed immigrants and ethnic peoples but did nothing to accommodate their oral preference. The pastor preached his same three-point sermon and used linear logic and reasoning to argue someone into seeing that they were a sinner in need of the gospel. More recently church planters, especially, are utilizing Chronological Bible Storying (CBS) and orality based discipleship methods to reach ethnic groups in the city.[20]

The purpose of this section is to consider orality issues in church planting and then provide a framework for developing contextualized orality strategies. First, I will discuss chronological Bible storying and its uses in urban ethnic contexts, focusing specifically on issues relating to worldview and language. Second, I will discuss the issue of secondary orality among immigrants who are very likely learning to read and write English, perhaps even in a formal ESL class. Third, I will discuss the limitations of orality strategies for sustaining healthy, reproducing churches.

Chronological Bible Storying

Tom Steffen notes that Bible storying is not just for those in rural villages. He finds features of orality and storying present in popular reality TV shows, soap operas, and talk shows (Steffen 2005: 19). These stories, even so called reality TV, are often made up and are not intended to convey any measure of truth. Rather, they are used for entertainment. However, stories command the attention of the hearer. While those in ministry are not in the entertainment business, stories can still be used to command attention. Chronological Bible Storying is a method of teaching the Bible that uses sequential narrative stories

---

[20]See for example Soma Church in the Northwest at www.wearesoma.com.

to reshape a people's faulty worldview with the truth of the biblical worldview. The key word in that sentence is worldview, which is the core framework for understanding and interpreting the world. Storying works because stories are already built into the culture of oral peoples as a key means of communicating information. CBS helps oral peoples to understand, remember, and retell key Bible stories.

The storying process. There are four essential steps to selecting which stories from Scripture to use in what is called a story set – a collection of biblical stories contextualized to the target people. First, the church planter must identify which stories from Scripture are essential to communicate salvific truth. Second, a worldview survey must be conducted to determine major bridges and barriers that exist in the people group's worldview. Additional stories are selected and added to the story set to address the specific worldview of the audience and help avoid syncretism. Third, the stories are crafted and delivered, often over a period of time. Fourth, hearers are asked to retell the story and the church planter can check for and correct errors and guide a discussion to aid the hearers' understanding and application of the story to their life.

Crafting the stories. First, the church planter should select key passages from Scripture that paint a picture of the broad salvific theme of the Bible. For example, select stories that iterate the nature of God, the created world, people, sin, sacrifice, restoration, Jesus, and repentance. These passages are universal for any culture to have a biblical understanding of God and his work in the world.[21]

Second, the church planter should consult the worldview identification research that has already been done and look for key worldview issues of the target people that have not already been addressed by the initial selection of Bible stories. Examples include finding stories that address spirit appeasement, the evil eye, luck, fate, fortune, destiny, ancestor veneration, karma, materialism, a relativistic approach to truth, and so on. If the church planter does not specifically address these worldview components, the target people will have no way of knowing their practices are sinful. They may believe in Jesus as a means of salvation, but be clueless as to how the gospel informs their understanding of spirit appeasement. Syncretism inevitably occurs when church planters do not address these issues that lay in what Paul Hiebert has called the "excluded middle." It is helpful to take a piece of paper and draw a line down the middle. On the left half, list key biblical foundations and research informed worldview flaws that must be addressed. On the right half, list passages from the Bible that address these issues. There is likely more than one passage that informs each issue. These passages will become the basis for the actual stories that are crafted next.

---

[21]See oralitystrategies.org for a fairly comprehensive listing of pre-made storysets that include these key biblical foundations as well as storysets for various cultural contexts.

Third, the stories themselves are crafted. The key is to bind each story so it has a clear beginning and ending and can function as a stand-alone story. Many Bible stories can be told just as they appear in the Scriptures. Others may need slight summarizing for clarity and/or length. Each story should be no more than about three minutes in length so it can be memorized and told. Large stories can be broken down into smaller components. Use simple words and short, direct sentences when writing out the story. Arrange the stories in chronological order.

Telling the stories. The hardest part of the whole process is actually memorizing and telling the stories in a compelling way. Western literates typically have poor memories and memorizing three minutes of story is difficult. My advice is to write the story out verbatim and then practice memorizing it until telling the story becomes natural and accurate. It usually takes several hours at least to memorize each story. Because of this time constraint, most oral teachers only introduce one new story a week. Perhaps your storying group meets every Tuesday evening. In this case, you have a week to memorize the next story. It is a good idea to begin each storying time by having someone retell the story from the past week to add continuity to the teaching.

When it is time to tell the story, it is important to set the stage and provide any biblical or cultural background that is necessary to understand the context of the story. Then, I begin with the words "This is a story from God's Word" in order to clearly divide my words and introduction from the sacred Scripture I am about to share so people aren't confused about what is from the Bible and what is my commentary on the passage. Then I tell the story in its entirety and finish with "This was a story from God's Word" to again bound the end of the story. Then I ask someone in the room to retell the story as best as they can. This is when it is important to have the story memorized so you, or someone from the group, can make corrections if the retelling isn't accurate. Then, I or someone from the audience tells the story again. Repetition is crucial for the memorization process and oral peoples expect a lot of repetition in their learning environment, even though this seems redundant to literates who are able to take notes and do not need repetition to recall information.

Finally, I have a discussion and application time focused on the story. This time will be most helpful if the church planter truly understands the culture of the people. Normal sermons in Western churches are twenty to forty minutes long and there is no discussion. However, such length is far too much for oral peoples to grasp well enough to remember. A three minute story might seem like "cheating" but in reality, they will remember the story well and the lengthy discussion and application time means they will have a "hook" to continually apply the truths to their lives.

Challenges in Urban Storying

A major issue for storying in the urban context is choosing which language to tell the stories in. Many agree that a native speaker using the group's heart language is best. But what if there are no believers in the target group and the church planters do not speak the language? Is English an acceptable substitute? After all, many immigrants are desperately trying to learn English already. Why not help their efforts by storying in English?

There are situations where there is little choice but to use English. When I was ministering to Nepali refugees in Louisville several years ago, there were no evangelical Christians in our Nepali community. None of us involved in church planting spoke Nepali. In another part of town there was a South Asian Indian storying group meeting. The stories were initially told in Hindi because it was assumed the majority of the people attending understood Hindi. It was discovered later that many of the Indians were straining to fully understand Hindi and more people actually understood English better than Hindi. For some of these immigrants, Hindi was their third or fourth language, while English was their second! The storying language was changed to English. In both cases it would be best to story in the heart language but in the first example, no believer knew Nepali and in the second example, there are so many heart languages represented in the group that it would not be feasible to story in them all. Such is the case in the multi-cultural urban context.

My team had a storyset recorded audibly in Nepali and transcribed in both Nepali and English. We told the story in English and the Nepalese read along. Then we played the story in Nepali so everyone could hear it in their own language. We told the story in English in addition to Nepali for two reasons. First, we could be better ensure the story was biblically accurate because we had a literal translation in English. Some groups will have a native speaker translate and tell the story but in that case, the church planters can never be certain the story remains faithful to Scripture. Syncretism can occur if incorrect words are substituted for biblical concepts (especially in light of their Hindu background) and the planter will be the last to know about it. The second reason we told the story in English is because the Nepalese wanted to learn English. Using the story in English helped them read along and hear American pronunciations.

This method was not without its problems, however. The Nepalese had a hard time remembering the story in English because their English skills were not very good. They could remember the story much better in Nepali but we had no believer equipped to follow up on the story in that language. We resorted to using the Nepali/English hybrid as a temporary solution. Our goal was to eventually bring in a Nepali believer to reinforce the story in Nepali and ask follow up comprehension and application questions.

The second issue for storying in diverse urban context is how to address worldview issues. In a mono-cultural setting, it is a matter of doing adequate field research to discover the worldview issues and then contextualize the story set to address needed issues. The same approach is necessary in the city, but the issue is vastly complicated by the diversity encountered in some neighborhoods or apartment complexes. My team sought to primarily plant a church among Nepalese who were Hindus. However, we often had Iraqi Muslims attend the conversation club because it was in the community room of their apartment complex. If both groups were present, we had to decide how to address polytheistic Hindus and monotheistic Muslims at the same time. When we showed that God is one, the Muslims cheered and the Hindus were offended. When we showed that God is "three persons," the Hindus cheered and the Muslims were offended. Such dilemmas went on and on.

The convictions of the church planter can bring clarity or confusion to situations like the one just described. Those who are comfortable starting mono-ethnic churches can story in the language and cater to the worldview most suited to the target people. Those attempting to plant multi-ethnic churches will have a more complex situation to address. One possibility is to story to the group using essential stories from Scripture in the common trade language but then to split the large group into smaller groups by language for the discussion time. This approach does not easily solve the issue, but may be one step in the right direction.

ESL and Secondary Orality

As stated numerous times throughout this book, immigrants to the United States are often exposed to or seek out ways to learn English, including learning to read and write. For example, my wife's Chinese boss first learned English by watching episodes of the David Letterman Show! However, introducing literacy to an oral background people involves much more than simply teaching them to read. The shift often requires an upheaval of their worldview. Ong notes that

> Oral cultures indeed produce powerful and beautiful verbal
> performances of high artistic worth. [However,] there is hardly an oral
> culture left in the world that is not somehow aware of the vast complex
> of powers forever inaccessible without literacy. This awareness is agony
> for persons rooted in primary orality, who want literacy passionately but
> who also know very well that moving into the world of literacy means
> leaving behind much that is deeply loved in the earlier oral world.
> [They] have to die to continue living (Ong 1982: 15).

Such language sounds strong, but the reality is that the introduction of literacy affects the entire worldview of oral peoples. Many first generation immigrants are caught between two worlds, especially regarding literacy. There are four areas that I will discuss to help church planters think about ministering to oral or oral preference learners who have come to the U.S.: residual orality, an oral worldview core, orality as a credible source for new information, and a hybrid approach to ministering to those who are residually oral.

First, the oral preference and key facets of the oral worldview do not immediately disappear when the people are exposed to literacy. This concept is called residual orality, and describes the persistence of oral learning and communication models even after the advent of literacy. Charles Kraft notes that people frequently "turn away from literacy because they *prefer* other forms of communication" (Kraft in the Preface to Klem 1982: *x*). Klem noticed in his own research and the research of others that reversion back into oral communication preferences is common among people just having learned to read and write. He notes that oral peoples could be taught to read quickly, but in less than a year, they had reverted back to orality. Why? Because they had no use for reading, did not practice it, and lost the ability to read and process information via print (Klem 1982: 14-17). This idea of reversion means that even immigrants from oral backgrounds who are taught to read, either in a refugee camp or ESL center upon arrival in the United States may still prefer oral means of communication. The oral wordview is tenacious and will likely never completely go away, especially among first generation immigrants.

Second, as alluded to above, even after learning to read and write, core worldview beliefs are still reinforced through culturally informed oral means. Hesselgrave states that in literate Asian societies, certain forms of drama are still a primary means to communicate religious and cultural values – worldview issues (Hesselgrave 1991: 550). In China, music is thought to have a power of its own and Confucian and Taoist teachings are common themes in Chinese opera. Similarly, in India, dance and drama are used to communicate the Jataka Tales, or birth stories about the Buddha. These art forms are more than mere entertainment. They are used to shape and reinforce the worldview of the people, bringing together the seen and unseen worlds and explaining the mysteries of origin, birth, sickness, death, good, evil, truth, and beauty (Ray 1971: 8). Furthermore, Chinese immigrants to cities in Malaysia bring their dance and theatre traditions. Chinese street opera is commonly found and often feature classics such as Romance of the Three Kingdoms, The Water Margin, and Madam White Snake (Koh and Ho 2009: 64). These examples show that even in diaspora contexts of literates living in urban centers, oral means of reinforcing worldview still prevail. Church planters in North America need to take advantage of the continued openness of immigrants to oral means of communicating worldview truths, which is the primary purpose of Chronological Bible Storying.

Third, oral communication methods add credibility and authority to the message, even in secondary oral contexts. As noted in Chapter 4, authority of the message is tied to the speaker who is known in the community. The relationship of the community with the teacher or speaker is as important as the actual features of the message itself (Rynkiewich 2007: 50-51). For the urban ethnic church planter, choosing to use an oral delivery method when preaching and teaching packages the information in a way that is credible for the people. It is essential he have a prolonged and close relationship with the people as well. For oral peoples, even residually oral peoples, relationship and communication method is what give credibility to the message, not the academic background of the church planter.

Fourth, a hybrid approach using both oral and literate means of evangelism, teaching, and training is likely the best overall approach when ministering in a secondary oral context in the United States. Church planters should begin using storying to gain credibility and start addressing worldview barriers to the gospel. Storying is a natural way to communicate information to oral peoples so they may be more receptive to a storying approach to the gospel than the use of gospel tracts or a syllogistic approach to evangelism where the evangelist attempts to logically reason the need for Jesus. The reality in the U.S. is that immigrants often do want to learn to read and write so, as I illustrated above, storying can be mixed with teaching ESL.

Soma's hybrid narrative preaching models.[22]

The Soma church network in the Northwest U.S. uses a hybrid orality approach in much of its preaching and discipleship. The church is successful at reaching college educated professionals and has found that this demographic responds well to alternate forms of preaching that still exposits the Scripture but is delivered in a variety of methods. Each of these models centers on telling a Bible story as described above, but the story is set in a more traditional preaching model. Soma describes five versions of narrative preaching, but I will here describe two examples that I use.

First is the "framed narrative sermon." Here, I set up the story by providing background and context and then actually tell my "points" up front to prime the people to listen for them in the story. Then, I tell the story in its entirety. Finally, this style of sermon finishes with reiterating the "points" and providing application. This method is effective because it lets the passage speak for itself, rather than the preacher breaking it up continually to provide explanation. People are drawn in to the story because I have already primed them for what to listen for.

The second method I use is called the "suspended narrative sermon." Here, I begin with the story but refrain from telling the ending. Then I make my points, exposition, and application and then close by telling the end of story as an exclamation to my points. This approach sets the stage and then builds

---

[22]The PDF document "Story of God Training" contains a description of all five models. This document and many other helpful resources, that serve as the basis for this section can be found at http://www.gcm_collec tive.org/article/story-of-god-training/

suspense to draw in the people. I leave them with the main point of the story because many researchers have found that people best remember the conclusion of a story or sermon.

These two and Soma's other three approaches to narrative preaching are effective because they package the Bible in a way that "sticks" with people so they can understand, remember, and later apply the passage to their lives. This is still expository preaching because it keeps the message of the passage intact and draws application directly from the passage. In fact, preaching this way may help people grasp the passage even better than other means of preaching so more of the Bible stays with the people long term.

Limitations of Oral Strategies

Oral strategies are a great tool for ethnic ministry in the U.S., but they carry certain limitations that must be discussed in an honest manner. There is some difficulty in transmitting oral theology across cultural contexts. Purely oral theology is housed in the songs, dances, poems, and stories of the culture. The personal and contextual nature of the theology does not carry well cross-culturally. A Muslim background community of Christ followers may have theology tied to purity, the obedience of Christ before the Father, and focus on Christ fulfilling the law. An animistic society may focus on themes such as Christ's power over demons. A group of believers from either culture would have difficulty transmitting their theological themes to the other culture. The question becomes, can an oral culture abstract their theology out of their local context in order to transmit it to a completely different context? Such contextualization may indeed be possible but it is difficult.

Next, a group's theological depth is only as deep as the amount of Scripture they have access to. Oral cultures are usually reached through Chronological Bible Storying (CBS) methods of evangelism and discipleship. One must remember that an oral culture does not have the luxury of reflecting on the entirety of Scripture. What they hear is all they know of the Bible. If the church planters develop a twenty four story set, then the theology derived from within those twenty four stories constitutes the entirety of what is available for further theological reflection. The largest story sets often do not contain more than one hundred stories. Again, the theological reflection and growth available to the people is directly tied to the body of Scripture they have access to. Apollos provides a good example of the limitation one encounters from not being able to access all of Scripture. Apollos knew the Scripture well and taught accurately, but he only had knowledge up to the baptism of John. Later, Apollos was instructed further in the Scriptures by Priscilla and Aquila (Acts 18: 24-26). If there were no Priscilla and Aquila, Apollos and, similarly, oral cultures would be left with a void in their theology.

What are leaders in an oral culture to do when they are left with a limited story set and they encounter theological issues their stories do not address, such as the beliefs of cults like Jehovah's Witnesses and Mormons? Hopefully, they have access to other more mature believers but if not, the situation could lead to syncretism. These limitations of oral theology are just that, limitations that must be considered. Orality strategies are essential for reaching oral and secondary oral people with the gospel. I believe they should be used as a bridge to written Scripture, however. Orality alone does not allow for sustained reflection on the whole of Scripture. Furthermore, the memories of oral peoples are not as reliable as some believe. The work of Lord, Parry, and Goody show that oral peoples memorize thematically rather than verbatim and have great difficulty retelling stories in the exact same way every time. Additionally, we rob people from other cultures of the full means for them to contribute to the growing field of global theology if we do not give people access to the full Scriptures.

Nonetheless, church planters must begin where the people are. Since two-thirds of the world's population prefers an oral approach to learning, we must take seriously the oral worldview. Storying and other orality strategies are the most appropriate way to begin ministering to oral peoples. The lost can hear and respond to the gospel and be gathered into churches. The ability of oral theology alone to sustain a healthy, reproducing church is to be questioned, however. More research needs to be done on the theology of congregations that have been exposed to limited story sets. CBS is, for good reason, the preferred method for reaching oral peoples today. CBS can be uncritically applied, however. The church at large must learn to live in the reality of the oral worldview, its limits, and the limits of our strategies in order to plant healthy churches. Failure to be honest about the limits of orality will inevitable result in a syncretized church. In order to further combat the encroachment of syncretism, I will now discuss the need to seat all that is done within the context of Hiebert's model of critical contextualization.

Critical Contextualization in the Urban, Ethnic Environment

Contextualization for the purposes of this book is defined as transmitting the truths of the Bible in a way that is biblically faithful and at the same time, culturally understandable. Hiebert asks the question, "How [should] missionaries respond to the traditional beliefs and practices of new converts?" (Hiebert 1994: 75). Essentially, how should a people marry, name their children, bury their dead, find spiritual fulfillment, and so on? Conversely, Hiebert explains that "the heart of the gospel must be kept by encoding it in forms that are understood by the people, without making the gospel captive to the [cultural] contexts" (Hiebert 2009: 29). Urban, ethnic church planting faces the issue of contextualization head on. Immigrants come with their cultural and religious history and encounter the gospel in the United States. As Chapter 5 showed, they are caught in the middle of two worlds and must determine how and to what extent they will assimilate. Church planters equipped with Hiebert's four step model for critical contextualization can help new believers think biblically about their old culture and how they can express their identity in a biblically faithful manner that preserves the God-given traits of their culture.

Step one requires what Hiebert calls an exegesis of the culture of the target people. The ethnographic research process described in Chapter 6 will aid the church planter in working with key informants from within the culture to best understand cultural identity and values here in North America. The worldview identification questionnaire is designed to address major cultural categories that are essential for helping plant a church that is not syncretized. It is important to understand the culture first so the church planter will know the general beliefs and practices with which to compare the Scriptures.

Step two requires the church planter and members of the new church to study the Scriptures together. The church planter must guide the process so that the church can read the Bible, or consider the Bible stories in a CBS model, as they were originally intended, or else the people will have a culturally distorted view of the Bible. The Scripture must be held in authority over the culture and function as the grid through which cultural practices are measured, or else biblical meanings will be forced to fit local cultural categories and distort the message.

Step three involves a critical response where both the church planter and the local believers evaluate their past customs in light of new biblical understandings and make decisions about the appropriateness of their cultural practices. Here, it is important for the church planter to let the local believers identify and admit to sinful cultural practices in light of the Scriptures. Such a process allows the people to grow in their ability to understand and apply the Bible to their lives. Additionally, if they themselves call for a change of cultural practices, the change is more likely to be accepted than if a foreigner demands the change. Syncretism is less likely to occur when the believers themselves identify sinful practices. The result of this critical study of cultural practices in light of the Scriptures is that many cultural practices will be retained because they are not inherently sinful. Other practices will be outright rejected because they are clearly sinful. Some practices may be seen as permissible, with slight modification. Finally, the people may need to create or adopt new customs to express biblical realities such as baptism that may not have been inherent to the old cultural ways.

Step four involves the process of adopting and practicing the new contextualized rituals. The intended goal is for the church's practices to be both biblically faithfully and culturally relevant. As the church lives and worships, both the church planter and the local believers need to provide ongoing checks against syncretism. Perhaps a new event occurs that the church has not yet thought of through a biblical lens. One example from my experience is the baby naming ceremony that Nepali Hindus have here in Louisville. The traditional practice is to consult the local priest who follows Hindu tradition and astrology to choose a name that gains the most favor from the gods. Nepalese who have become believers are often troubled about whether they can name their children in this fashion. Walking them through Hiebert's model of critical contextualization provides biblical insight into this important cultural practice.

Hiebert describes the value of his approach to contextualization in five points (Hiebert 1994: 91-92). 1) It takes the authority of the Bible seriously as the rule for faith and life. 2) It recognizes the work of the Holy Spirit in the lives of all believers to discern truth. 3) The church acts as a hermeneutical community rather than the pastor or church planter making all of the decisions. This point is especially important in oral cultures, where the community is regularly involved in the decision making and enforcement process. 4) This model allows for a global discussion of theology where those from other cultures are afforded the opportunity to see Scripture through their cultural lens. However, those trained in theology and hermeneutics are also present to guide the process. 5) It views contextualization as an ongoing process where the community is continually evaluating its practices according to the authority of the Scriptures and the Lordship of Christ.

One can see the difficulties of doing critical contextualization in a completely oral context. As noted above, one limitation of CBS is a limited storyset. How are believers able to evaluate all of their cultural practices against the Scriptures if they do not have access to the entirety of the Bible? The church planter can help in this situation, but too much outside assistance in theologizing can begin to create a dependency issue. However, if church planters do not have a deep enough understanding of the culture or a keen enough understanding of the Scripture, syncretism may creep in. I know of one ethnic church plant in Chicago that retained many cultural practices of the target people. So much so that other pastors in the community from the same ethnic group were suspicious that people were being led astray. Eventually, those other ethnic pastors came and persuaded the members to abandon the church because it had become syncretized. Church planting in urban, ethnic contexts is complex. I have described key issues related to the task, including deciding whether to plant a mono or multi-ethnic church, handling orality issues in an urban context, and critically contextualizing the gospel. I now turn to mobilizing the church at large to complete the task.

Training Churches and Developing Partnerships

Cities are diverse ethnically and culturally. Most cities, especially in the U.S. are also diverse ecclesiologically. Large cities have large numbers of churches. Some of these churches desire to reach the ethnic groups that are at their door steps. The task is far too large for one church. Churches must work together to share resources, strategies, and people to accomplish the Great Commission. However, mobilizing and training churches to reach ethnic groups in the city requires a number of important issues be addressed, specifically those cross-cultural issues inherent to ethnic church planting.

Training Churches

Horror stories abound where well-meaning churches made serious cultural faux pauxs while attempting to reach immigrants. I know of a recent cultural festival put on by the city of Louisville. The event attracted hundreds of immigrants and refugees. One well-meaning church sent a team to the event to share the gospel. The church's evangelism van pulled up and six members emerged and gathered a group of Nepalese around them. The team began telling the Nepalese they must believe in Jesus right now or else they would go to Hell. Much to the church members' delight, all of the Nepalese professed faith and signed a card indicating their decision. The team moved around the festival using similar evangelistic methods all day, and with similar results. A few weeks later several members of that church attended a Nepali story group where ethnic church planters had been faithfully laying a foundation for the gospel for months. The visiting church members derided the church planters and told them all they need to do is preach about Hell and the Nepalese will repent, just as they had at the cultural festival. Little did these church members realize, but none of the "decisions for Christ" the Nepalese made were genuine. They had only gone along with the show in order to not be embarrassed by saying no to the evangelists who obviously wanted a certain response.

Without training, churches will begin reaching ethnic groups on their own initiative and according to their own perceived best method. These churches can sometimes do more harm than good, however. It is crucial that those trained in cross-cultural ministry provide training sessions for other churches in the city. In Louisville, churches have workshops on worldview identification and Chronological Bible Storying every few months. Training is offered to individual churches who desire to reach ethnic groups in their neighborhoods. Ethnic church planters attend associational meetings and ecumenical gatherings in order to find out which churches want to reach ethnic groups and to offer cross-cultural training to these churches. Just as missionaries preparing for the field receive in depth training, so must local churches that are crossing cultural boundaries with the gospel. Providing cross-cultural training also begins to address a second question – that of how to develop city wide partnerships between churches reaching ethnic groups.

Mobilization and Developing Partnerships

Even in a relatively small city like Louisville with a metro population of around one million, it is difficult to know of all the efforts being made to reach ethnic groups. Many resources are not being used efficiently because churches are not connected. Some churches have no access to helpful resources while others are targeting the same neighborhoods unaware of each other's efforts. Recently there was a Nepali dinner fellowship in another part of the city that I was unaware of until the day it happened. I had no time to invite my Nepali friends who live in a different part of the city. In order to avoid such situations, a networking system has been developed on Facebook called "people groups Louisville" in order to provide information and resources for those in the city doing ethnic church planting. In addition, a new interdenominational networking group has been formed that meets bi-monthly.[23] The very first meeting had over fifty people attend from various churches. Several of us were surprised to hear of others who were attempting a similar ministry to Nepalese in town that we had never heard about. These meetings are intended to provide prayer, encouragement, opportunity, and resources for anyone reaching ethnic groups in the city. We passed a sheet around that asked each person to name one other person who might be interested in a partnership. We hope to slowly build a base that will allow for healthy networking, training opportunities, and partnerships.

One major benefit of a network is the ability to share resources. For example, the Nepali story set my team used originated with a missionary in Nepal. A student at The Southern Baptist Theological Seminary knew the missionary and asked for the story set to use with a Nepali ministry in Louisville. I found out about this ministry and asked for the story set to use in the community I ministered in. At the networking meeting mentioned above, I discovered another church who was attempting to reach Nepali refugees in their neighborhood but did not have a story set and were not familiar with CBS. The networking meeting allowed me to both pass on the story set and also to offer training to use it properly. There are several groups in Louisville reaching out to Iraqi refugees. No one had a Creation to Cross story set in Iraqi Arabic. We agreed to combine resources and personnel in Louisville and write and record an Iraqi Arabic story set. Once the story set was finished, we could offer it to other groups in town doing a similar ministry.

It may seem obvious that churches need training in cross-cultural ministry and that networking and partnerships are helpful. Many cities have no such

---

[23]Many of these efforts are coordinated by a ministry called Refuge Louisville. See refugelouisville.com.

partnerships, however, or they are ineffective. We all need to be reminded and challenged to give time and resources to developing training and other tools to help the gospel reach more people in our cities. Creating a Facebook page is a simple first step. Hosting multiple networking and training sessions throughout the year is even better. Sometimes all it takes is one or two people to step forward and organize an event and good follow up can ensure future effectiveness.

Indigenous Leadership Development

Reaching and raising up local leadership has been the goal in international missions for many years. However, the same mentality is not always shared in U.S. churches. Most churches, when they need a pastor, look to a seminary or their denomination for a "ready made" leader. Some of these churches have concluded that to be successful, they need an "A+" caliber leader, and recruit until they find one. This is a sad contrast to the New Testament's emphasis on making disciples, mentoring, and equipping the saints for the work of the ministry. Healthy, biblical churches reach people with the gospel, disciple them, and raise them to leadership within their own congregation.[24]

This approach is especially crucial for urban, ethnic ministry. Often, the language barrier alone requires that a local person be equipped to pastor his own ethnic group. Additionally, ethnic communities often respond better to leadership from someone they know and already trust. Importing an outsider can send a message that locals aren't good enough or can cause cultural problems that may have been unforeseen. Locals already know the community and have the relational capital that is crucial in ethnic ministry. Planting a church that is geared toward evangelism, discipleship, and continued church planting is only possible when local leaders are continually raised up. When we begin to see the people around us as possible leaders, our entire approach to ministry can change.

As Conn and Ortiz point out, indigenous leaders have a number of characteristics outsiders do not share (Conn and Ortiz 2001: 382-83). They already see their city as home; there is no need to convince them of the needs and opportunities. They know how to survive in the city, know the dangers, know the noise and stress, and know the limits of what has already been done.

Ethnic ministry leadership development is best done through an apprenticeship style training. Books and classes do not fit the context of many ethnic communities. Rather, a church planter should take on a small group of prospective leaders and take them with him as he ministers in the city. They

---

[24]This topic could, and probably should, constitute an entire chapter. However, Conn and Ortiz have already devoted over one-hundred pages to this topic in their excellent book *Urban Ministry* and we can add little to their recommendations there. We will only highlight a few major issues of which to be made aware.

can help with community research and evangelism, they can assist in sermon preparation or Bible story development to learn those skills, and they can disciple men and women of their own. This hands on approach to ministry training builds their character as well as their skills as they watch the church planter and encounter teachable moments in regular life and learn to apply the gospel to every situation. This method is most natural for many ethnic peoples to learn and is the most transferable to their culture and context.

Summary

This chapter has covered a number of key issues in urban, ethnic ministry. Significant challenges include the mono or multi-ethnic church discussion, reaching oral peoples, contextualization, church mobilization and training, and indigenous leadership development. Now that we have laid a general foundation on the nature of immigration in the U.S., major assimilation strategies and patterns, worldview and cultural research, and addressed key issues in urban ministry, we can finally turn to presenting a strategy to minister in each of the three patterns of assimilation that takes into account all we have covered.

PART 4

DIASPORA MISSIOLOGY
IN ACTION

CHAPTER 8

DIASPORA MISSIOLOGY: AN INTRODUCTION

Introduction

To those readers might not be familiar with the term and concept of "diaspora missiology," and this chapter is a general overview written for them.

The New Reality of Christian Missions in the 21st Century

There are two phenomena contributing to the change of reality of Christian missions in the 21st century: intensive and extensive movement of people globally and the epic shift of the center of gravity of Christianity. Mass movement of people caused by war, famine, and natural and human catastrophes happened quite regularly. However, the scale and intensity of the movement of people globally in the 21st century are unprecedented in scale and intensity due to the confluence of forces created by modernization, urbanization, and globalization.

Christian missions are to be carried out wherever people are being found, therefore, this new reality requires us to have a new orientation and approach in Christian missions, leading to the emergence of "diaspora missiology."

With the decline of Christianity in Europe and North America where for centuries missionaries originated, western countries in the 21st century are now mission fields. Many cathedrals in Europe with historical and architectural significance are now relics and tourist sites. Even the current Pope of the catholic church worldwide is no longer from Europe; but from South

America. As Philip Jenkins and Andrew Walls[25] have pointed out that there is the shifting of Christendom's center of gravity from the west to the rest and from the northern hemisphere to the south.

Diaspora Missiology as an Emerging Missiological Framework

"Diaspora missiology" recently has emerged to become a new missiological framework in the context of two global demographic trends of the 21st century: "the phenomenon of large scale diaspora and followed by the shifting of Christendom's center of gravity from the west to the rest and from the northern hemisphere to the southern hemisphere." (Wan 2014:6)[26]

The term "diaspora" is a derivation from the Greek word "*diaspeirein*" which means "to scatter about" and is a reference to "people moving away from their homeland" including refugees and immigrants. "Diaspora missiology" is "a missiological framework for understanding and participating in God's redemptive mission among diaspora groups."[27]

Theory and Practice of Diaspora Missiology

As shown in the table below, there are two types of "diaspora ministry" and four types of "diaspora missions" within the framework of diaspora missiology. "Diaspora ministry" is defined as: "serving the diaspora in the name of Jesus Christ and for His sake in these two ways: (1) ministering to the diaspora, i.e., serving the diaspora, and (2) ministering through the diaspora, i.e., mobilizing the diaspora to serve others." (Wan 2014:5) "Diaspora missions" is defined as: Christians' participation in God's redemptive mission to evangelize their kinsmen on the move, and through them to reach out to natives in their homelands and beyond.[28]

---

[25] Philip Jenkins, *The Next Christendom: The Coming of Global Christianity*, 2001; Walls Andrew F. (1996) *The Missionary Movement in Christian History: studies in the transmission of faith*, Maryknoll, Ny: Orbis.

[26] Enoch Wan, Diaspora Missiology: Theory, Methodology and Practice, IDS-USA, 2014 (2nd ed.)
[27] See "The Seoul Declaration on Diaspora Missiology," accessed March 25, 2010; available at http://www.lausanne.org/documents/seoul-declaration-on-diaspora-missiology.html.
[28] Enoch Wan, "Global People and Diaspora Missiology," presentation at Plenary session, Tokyo 2010-Global Mission Consultation, Tokyo, Japan, May 13, 2010.

Table 2. Diaspora missiology: diaspora ministry & diaspora missions
(Wan 2014:8)

DIASPORA MISSIOLOGY		DIASPORA MINISTRY			
	Type	ministering **to** the diaspora		ministering **along** the diaspora	
	Means	the Great Commandment as pre-evangelistic and holistic		the Great Commission – imperative and inclusive	
	Recipient	focusing on diaspora: serving the diaspora by ministering - social and spiritual dimensions		focusing beyond diaspora: mobilizing diaspora Christians to serve other diaspora people or non-diaspora	
		DIASPORA MISSIONS			
	Type	missions **to** the diaspora	missions **through** the diaspora	missions **by** & **beyond** the diaspora	missions **with** the diaspora
	Means	motivate & mobilize diaspora individuals & congregations to partner with others: the Great Commission, i.e. evangelistic outreach, discipleship, church planting and global missions			
	Recipient	focusing on diaspora		focusing beyond diaspora	
		members of diaspora community	kinsmen in homeland & elsewhere; not cross-culturally	cross-culturally to other ethnic groups in host society and beyond	partnership between diaspora and others in Kingdom ministry

There are four types of diaspora missions (Wan 2014:6)

1. **Missions *to* the Diaspora** — reaching the diaspora groups in forms of evangelism or pre-evangelistic social services, then disciple them to become worshipping communities and congregations.

2. **Missions *through* the Diaspora** — diaspora Christians reaching out to their kinsmen through networks of friendship and kinship in host countries, their homelands, and abroad.

3. **Missions *by* and *beyond* the Diaspora** — motivating and mobilizing diaspora Christians for cross-cultural missions to other ethnic groups in their host countries, homelands, and abroad.

4. **Missions *with* the Diaspora** — mobilizing non-diasporic Christians individually and institutionally to partner with diasporic groups and congregations.

Diaspora missiology is an emerging ministry strategy among evangelical circles. According to J.D. Payne, contemporary migration patterns is a "Great Commission opportunity" in which the God of all Nations is "working out his will in the universe" (Payne 2012: 30); especially for the church in the West to strategically bring the gospel to immigrants in urban centers (or the "strangers next door") without ever leaving the United States.[29]

Summary

This chapter begins with a description of two global demographic trends of the 21st century: the extensive and intensive moving of people from their homeland and the shifting of Christendom's center of gravity from the west to the rest and from the northern hemisphere to the south.

The "diaspora missiology" is introduced as the emerging missiological framework in response to the new reality of Christian missions in the 21st century. Then definitions and explanations of diaspora ministry and diaspora mission are provided for the reader, in anticipation of the subsequent chapters showing diaspora missiology in action; especially in urban contexts of major cities in the U.S.

---

[29] Payne JD. (2012) *Strangers next door : immigration, migration, and mission,* Downers Grove, Ill.: IVP Books.

CHAPTER 9

DIASPORA MISSIOLOGY IN ACTION

Introduction

This chapter is the application of previous chapters and presents general strategies for reaching people in each of the three assimilation patterns presented in Chapter 5. These strategies are grounded in research, but should not be seen as a one size fits all model. Feel free to use them as a starting point and adapt to the specific needs in your context.

Assimilation Pattern Strategies

Chapter 5 revealed that immigrants primarily settle into one of three patterns of assimilation in North America. These assimilation patterns are largely dependent on the background of the immigrant group and whether they possess human capital or social capital. Human capital refers to high levels of English proficiency, college education or higher, professional job skills, and a long term commitment to living in the United States. Social capital refers more to the relational network of immigrants that provides them the means to get to the U.S. and find employment even with low levels of English proficiency, minimal technical job skills, and little education.

The first assimilation pattern is the ethnic enclave where immigrants of the same or similar cultural backgrounds group into a geographically dense section of the city and rely on an ethnically driven local economy. In the enclave, little assimilation is required because immigrants are able to speak their native language in both the home and the workplace. Ethnic enclaves are primarily composed of immigrants with high levels of social capital rather than human capital so they are more dependent on the enclave environment for survival in their new setting.

A second pattern of assimilation is the cultural threads model where immigrants of the same ethnic group do not live in close geographic proximity but are closely linked through a variety of social networks. This phenomenon is described as heterolocalism, defined as "recent populations of shared ethnic identity which enter an area from distant sources, then quickly adopt a dispersed pattern of residential location, all the while managing to remain cohesive through a variety of means" (Zelinksy and Lee 1998: 281). These immigrants have high levels of human capital such as financial, educational, and business resources and often place job consideration as a higher priority than geographic location near members of their own ethnic group. However, they remain closely connected through internet communities, ethnic business associations, ethnic shopping malls, food stores, restaurants, places of worship, and cultural festivals that serve as worldview and cultural intensifiers in the community. The cultural threads model requires more assimilation than an enclave environment but most immigrants continue to possess a deeper ethnic identity than is immediately visible at the surface level.

A final model of assimilation found in North America is what I describe as the urban tribe model. Some cultural anthropologists state that as globalization increases and cities become more multi-cultural, people need to find their identity in smaller communities (Hiebert and Meneses 1995: 267). In a diverse urban setting, some people group according to affinity rather than ethnic identity. For example, an ethnically diverse group of college students in New York City share similar socio-economic background, the English language, and all study anthropology so they find more in common with each other than perhaps with other people in the city from their ethnic group with whom they have little contact. Some missiologists are proposing that urban tribes can be reached as a distinct "tribe" in the city and church planters do not have to take into account the unique ethnic and cultural background of each individual in the group. In some regards, the urban tribe model requires the highest level of assimilation because individuals are thought to drop or severely downplay their cultural identity and form a new identity in a multi-cultural setting.

Each of these three models of assimilation requires a different approach for evangelism and church planting. The addition of orality issues further complicates the task of the church planter. Drawing from research presented in previous chapters, we will propose church planting strategies for each model that should be effective based on the specific dynamics present in each model. These are only suggestions and are meant to be a starting point for ministry. Local research should shape these suggestions further so the church best matches the context. For each model, we describe five areas the church planter will need to address: 1) entry into the community, 2) language most essential for ministry, 3) common felt needs used to build relationships and bridge to church planting, 4) importance of using orality strategies, and 5) model of church.[30] As stated above, each church planter must also have the skills to conduct field research to ascertain the specific worldview and cultural identity of his target population.

---

[30]For an overview of various models of church, see J. D. Payne, *Discovering Church Planting: An Introduction to the Whats, Whys, and Hows of Global Church Planting* (Colorado Springs: Paternoster, 2009), 309-24.

Reaching the Ethnic Enclave Community

In some ways, enclaves are as close as an immigrant can get to replicating his or her home culture. Enclaves are composed of a high density ethnic population often generating some kind of niche economy in the city. These communities are small cities within the larger city. For these reasons, finding an enclave of immigrants is not difficult in a city. In fact, many large enclaves are touted as tourist destinations in cities like Chicago, New York, Los Angeles, and San Francisco. However, real people live and die beyond the tourist shops at the outer fringe of the community and these people need the gospel.

Gaining access to those in the enclave is a significant challenge. Outsiders are welcome in the tourist shops, but the dynamics of an enclave create a suspicion of outsiders. Additionally, enclaves typically have a hierarchically structured leadership system that governs decisions for the community and enforces protocol. Many enclaves make it unnecessary for members to learn English so the immigrant's native language is likely to remain dominant. These features of enclaves must be taken into account when attempting to plant churches in these unique communities.

First, because of the closed nature of the enclave community, it is essential that the church planter find cultural insiders to work with. The ethnographic research process described in Chapter 6 should reveal a number of key informants who could then become the gateway for the entry of the gospel. Enclaves require significant time to build relationships and gain acceptance and credibility. Helping people understand that you are there for their good and not just looking for illegal immigrants can go a long way. Insiders can introduce you and provide that initial credibility on your behalf. Additionally, the church needs to be located inside the community since enclaves often contain everything the community needs for survival such as grocery stores, banks, and schools.

Second, ministry ought to be done in the native language if possible. For example, in the Manhattan Chinatown, the Fuzhounese dialect is used across the enclave both in the home and in public. The very draw of the enclave for immigrants is that they do not need to assimilate or learn English in order to find jobs and survive in the United States. It may be impossible for outside church planters to learn the local language here in the U.S. In this case, it is even more important to find locals who are bilingual and train them to be the church planter. Another possible strategy that some mission agencies have begun trying is to station missionaries on furlough in cities with large populations of people from the missionary's ministry since the missionary will already know the language. The short nature of missionary furloughs still requires an immediate focus on finding and raising up local leadership who can speak the language.

Third, felt needs will be different in the enclave. Common needs based approaches to ethnic ministry include teaching English, helping immigrants study for the U.S. citizenship exam, and teaching immigrants to drive in the U.S. However, learning English may not be essential in the enclave so ESL clubs might not be an effective means to draw people. There is often a high level of illegal immigrants in the enclave so some individuals will not want to be identified and work toward citizenship. Enclaves in large cities may have access to public transportation so immigrants may not even own a car so driving lessons would not be attractive. Effective strategies may include helping immigrants adjust to the new environment through temporary housing, especially in enclaves where immigrants are commonly exploited. If a church can rent several apartments inside the enclave neighborhood, they can advertise the space in local shops and ethnic websites as a transition for new arrivals. Church planters can then use the apartment as a place to begin ministry, connect with others in the enclave, and provide a needed service to the community that builds rapport. Furthermore, church planters can either provide space or help immigrants find space to develop community gardens where native foods can be grown. My study of Nepali refugees living in a loose enclave in Louisville found that the community gardens at their apartment complex provided a place for cultural reinforcement in the midst of pressure to change. The gardens were a good place to meet with and talk to refugees about their lives and use the worldview identification worksheet listed in Appendix 1.

Fourth, because enclaves require little assimilation or change from the old worldview and way of life, it is likely that immigrants will be much closer to the pre-literate end of the orality spectrum. Chronological Bible Storying will be a necessary and helpful approach to begin ministry, as enclave immigrants are more likely to retain their oral worldview. Storying is a non-threatening and familiar means to begin introducing biblical truth. Additionally, individuals who attend a storying group can share the stories with others in their community easily since they all live in close proximity.

Fifth, a house church model may be more effective in an enclave environment for several reasons. One is the high cost of renting or buying a standing church building in the larger cities in the U.S. that house true ethnic enclaves. Rent for space for a church in Manhattan regularly runs in the tens of thousands a month! Few churches in the country can afford those prices. Additionally, the highly relational nature of many immigrants means that a house church could be more inviting and less threatening and foreign than a free standing church building. Enclave residents are not as likely to leave their community to attend church in an unfamiliar part of the city. Finally, the house church model is more easily reproducible and may be able to spread more quickly in a densely populated enclave neighborhood.

Reaching the Cultural Thread Community

The key dynamic of the cultural thread model of assimilation is its heterolocality. Individuals from the ethnic group live in a geographically diverse area but remain culturally connected. They possess a collective cultural consciousness that binds them together with other members of their people group. Members of these communities remain connected through business associations, cultural festivals, places of worship, and through internet communities. These centers of cultural exchange provide a place for cultural reinforcement in the midst of a diverse society that attempts to pull the immigrants into mainstream America. The community comes together many times a year to reinforce their worldview and cultural identity, along with their right to be different in the midst of American mainstream culture.

First, the difficulty in reaching these types of communities is that they do not appear to be connected and it can be difficult to access members within the community. The research methods presented in Chapter 6 for finding "hidden peoples" are likely to be necessary to locate individuals from the target people group. Church planters should identify and follow the network threads to build relationships and gain access to the community. Immigrants assimilating in the cultural thread model often have high levels of human capital so they may be more receptive to ESL clubs and other classes that help them prepare to become fully integrated U.S. citizens. Church planters should visit the local ethnic stores, restaurants, and cultural festivals to build relationships. One could post advertisements for ESL and other classes in these establishments, as was common in the Brazilian ethnic stores I visited during my research in London. In some U.S. cities, ethnic communities have begun publishing newspapers in their language. These papers are also key places to both find when and where people are meeting and to advertise classes, as immigrants rarely prefer getting their news from U.S. based papers and keep in touch with their home culture through these ethnic publications.

Second, the most appropriate language for ministry would depend on the needs of the people as discovered through research. If important cultural reinforcers like worship, festivals, and celebrations are done in the native language, it is likely the church planter would need to share the gospel in the same language. These events reveal issues at the worldview level and language is often key to changing worldview. It may be that English is preferable if immigrants are fluent and use the language in their everyday lives and interactions with both insiders and outsiders. However, one must be cautious to avoid making the assumption that since English is commonly used, it is appropriate for ministry and to address worldview level beliefs. It may be that there is a distinct split between cultural identity in the public and private life of these immigrants where English is used in public but the mother tongue is used in the home.

Third, felt needs for immigrants linked via the cultural thread model often center on tools needed for assimilation into mainstream culture, at least publically and for children. Approaches that may be successful based on the dynamics of these communities include programs to help immigrants learn three essentials for success in the United States: learning English, learning to drive, and passing the citizenship exam. Additionally, church planters could host workshops to help new immigrant businessmen learn the specific tax laws and approaches to starting a business in the United States and provide continued coaching in these endeavors. Furthermore, tutoring services targeted at the children of these immigrants can help them excel in school and gain access to quality colleges and universities in the U.S. Cultural threads model immigrants have a long term perspective so they are likely to be heavily invested in learning the intricacies of American culture.

Fourth, many of these immigrants are likely to be literate so a fully oral approach to ministry may not be effective. A hybrid approach as described in Chapter 7 and created by Soma Community Church may be more appropriate.[31] Soma describes five models of preaching that can be adapted for evangelism or storying groups with immigrant communities. The models provide varying amounts of pure story mixed with exposition and application of the text, depending on the needs of the target community. Storying provides a non-threatening approach to begin talking about spiritual matters so it could be useful as a bridge with those closer to the literate end of the orality spectrum. However, businessmen will be more familiar with and accustomed to literate means of communication. However, even immigrants with graduate degrees and professional careers may respond better to a more oral based approach to worldview transformation since core elements of their own worldview are still likely reinforced through story, poems, and dramas.

Fifth, the style of church most appropriate for a dispersed immigrant community would depend on research findings within the community. Perhaps many from this community would prefer to attend church with other Americans at an established church that has programs for their children. These immigrants are likely used to driving long distances from their homes to their places of employment so driving a distance to a church would not be a problem, as it would in the enclave community. One must not force the house church model on all immigrant peoples because in some cases, such a model could actually repel people who would be more comfortable in an established church building.

A key danger for those working with the cultural threads model is overlooking functional assimilation. This is where immigrants adopt mainstream cultural traits and skills to excel in public and especially in the workplace. Think of the "go along to get along" mentality. They have the skills to integrate in the workplace and can appear to have greatly lowered their own cultural identity. However, the private life of these immigrants can be drastically different. At home, they speak their heart language and express their worldview and identity similarly to people in their home culture. Hindu Indians are especially likely to functionally assimilate and are even known to call themselves Christians at work. However, their pluralistic worldview is just below the surface and no real change has taken place. It is important with anyone, but especially with immigrants in the cultural threads model, for the church planter to attempt to know individuals holistically in public and private life.

Reaching the Urban Tribe Community

The theory of the urban is tribe is based on diverse individuals who find a common affinity that provides identity and community in the midst of a "faceless" urban environment. The linking affinity can be status as a refugee, students in an ESL class, parents of children attending the same school, ethnic business entrepreneurs, college students, and many more. Some research may indicate that tribal groups will move "up" a level in their ethnic identity when they immigrate. Yorubas are willing to identity just as Nigerians or even West Africans in the United States and may affiliate with other Nigerian tribal groups that may have been traditional enemies in Nigeria. In some ways, the urban tribe model is an over assimilation as individuals go beyond mainstream culture and form a new and distinct identity revolving around affinity and sub-culture.

First, entry into the urban tribe community may be difficult. Unless individuals live in college housing or a refugee dominated apartment complex, finding individuals will be a challenge. Those desiring to reach ethnic peoples in the urban tribe assimilation model probably do not have a single ethnic group as their target people since the very nature of the urban tribe theory is to drop core ethnic identity and find identity in an affinity. Entry into the community would likely come through entering the affinity that bonds the group together. Since the group is already diverse, suspicion of outsiders may not be strong, as long as the outsider has a legitimate reason to seek entry into the "tribe." For example, if the church planter has no business skills or experience, it would not be the best idea to attempt to join a business association just to gain access to ethnic peoples. If they church planter really does share a love for the uniting affinity, then it should be easy to relate to others in that same affinity.

Second, the ministry language by nature must be one shared by all members of the group. This may be English in the United States. However, it may also be a trade language of the country of origin if the "tribe" is composed of individuals from the same country or region. For example, many immigrants to the U.S. from Mexico are actually tribal peoples from southern Mexico. Their preferred language may be their respective tribal language but in the U.S., they speak Spanish with each other and have formed an urban tribe. Similarly, there are many Nepali and Bhutanese refugees in the United States. There are more than one hundred and twenty languages in Nepal, though most also speak Nepali as the trade language. Nepali refugees in the U.S. speak Nepali with each other, but if they find speakers of their tribal language, they prefer to use that language. One ethnic pastor recommends ministering in the heart language if possible but notes that the most important thing is the sincerity of the church planter and time spent building relationships with the people, regardless of the language.

Third, felt needs vary depending on the nature of the "tribe." Refugees living together in an apartment complex often desire to learn English, gain job skills, learn to drive, and eventually become U.S. citizens. For example, I conducted a research project to determine why Nepali refugees were having trouble getting jobs. I discovered that in Nepali culture, it is rude to "put one's self forth" in an interview setting. In U.S. culture, employers expect interviewees to prove why they are ideal for the job. Essentially, there was a clash of cultural values. I then conducted a resume building and interview skills workshop at the apartment complex and had the Nepalis role play job interviews to become more comfortable in that setting. Internationals in a college urban tribe setting would have different felt needs so individual research must be conducted to determine the best ministry approach.

Fourth, the need for an orality based ministry will also vary widely depending on the background of those in the urban tribe. I used a mixed approach when ministering to refugees who were in the process of learning to read and write English. I began a class by telling a Bible story in English so the refugees could hear native pronunciation. They could also read along with the story to improve reading skills. I had the same story set recorded in Nepali and would then play the story in Nepali. Someone would attempt to retell the story in either English or Nepali. Next, I would teach an English lesson based on vocabulary from the story. Finally, I broke the group into smaller groups and would have a conversation and discussion time centered on the story to help with story comprehension and also to give the refugees time to practice English. College students or businessmen with advanced levels of English may not respond as well to an orality based ministry. Church planters should use the orality survey tool in Appendix 2 in order to determine the most appropriate approach in their specific ministry context.

Fifth, the model of church will also vary depending on the context. Refugees may not have a car, or feel comfortable traveling to other areas of the city. In my case, we used the community room at the apartment complex because the area was neutral, easily accessible, and free of charge. When I helped with a church plant for international university students, we met on campus so students could walk to church and easily invite their friends. Church planters must conduct research to discover the best location and venue for the church to meet in, taking into account cost, group dynamics regarding insider and outsider mentality, and accessibility.

Urban tribe immigrant groups are also susceptible to functional assimilation without any real worldview change. The nature of this model is diversity so it is perhaps the most difficult to recommend a strategy for reaching the urban tribe.

Summary

The overarching theme regarding strategy in each of the three assimilation models is the need for specific research. General patterns and predictions have been made and strategies suggested that will likely fit the models, but as this entire book has attempted to show, there is no one size fits all strategy for reaching ethnic groups in the city. Church planters can use recommendations from this chapter as a framework to conduct their own research and create the most appropriate and contextualized approach for ministry in their specific context.

CHAPTER 10

CONCLUSION AND CHALLENGE

Cities and urban living are quickly coming into vogue in the United States. The white flight of the mid-20th century is reversing and city centers and old urban neighborhoods are being repopulated and revitalized. This influx is good for the city in many ways. U.S. cities are again places of life and vitality and it is good to see old abandoned warehouses, school buildings, and factories transformed into places of cultural production. In some ways, the U.S. church has been behind the curve to make efforts to reach the city again. Thankfully, this mentality is changing, and changing rapidly, especially with younger Christians. Cities are strategic places for ministry, especially ethnic ministry. Churches must be aware, however, that ministry in the city is not the same as ministry in the suburbs or in small towns. Churches cannot simply import twenty people from their suburban congregation and expect to plant healthy, growing inner city churches.

As this book has shown, the city must be understood on its own terms. Large urban areas exert external pressure on residents through government zoning, housing laws, and resettlement plans that result in the divided city. Immigrants, especially, cannot just live wherever they want. If they come as refugees they are funneled into government approved housing. If they come with little human capital, they are reliant on their social network and may funnel into an enclave environment. Even those who have the financial means to choose where they live still find themselves connected to their people through their heterolocal communal culture. Assimilation patterns and settlement strategies play a role in cultural identity and expression of immigrant peoples. The complexity of these relationships cannot be overstated. But many find the complexity of the city to be one of the most refreshing and inviting features of urban life and ministry.

In many ways, urban ministry must be thought of as a new mission field that requires all the same preparation as those going overseas undertake. Urban ethnic church planters need ethnographic research skills to find and learn about the specifics of their people in the city. Dynamics of language, worldview, orality background, and suspicion of outsiders make ethnic ministry difficult. But, when approached with humility, the mentality of a learner, prayer, and reliance on God, urban ministry can be one of the most rewarding endeavors.

The city is too large a place for churches to operate in isolation from one another. Partnerships and cooperation are essential. New church plants have much to learn from others who have struggled in the city for years. Those older churches need the refreshment, excitement, vision, and even the naivety of those new churches to remember their own initial excitement for urban ministry. It is arrogant for any one church to believe they have ministry figured out and no longer need to learn from and work with others. God is building his kingdom, even in the city, and he does not do it through one church.

As we come to a close, be encouraged and hopeful. It is our prayer that this book will be useful as you step into God's calling on your life to care for his people in the city. We don't have urban ministry figured out and so look to you to make your contribution to the U.S. church. Share your research, insights, successes, and failures with others. Go to conferences, publish articles, and speak passionately about the needs, difficulty, and beauty of urban ministry. Be an advocate for immigrants in your community, learn from them, seek to bless them, and be blessed by them.

Finally, seek the peace of the city, plant your life there, raise your children there, multiply there both physically and spiritually and do not decrease. Pray to the Lord on your city's behalf, for in its welfare you will find your welfare (Jer. 29:5-7). Though Israel was exiled because of their sin, God called them to live fully where he planted them and to build the Kingdom there. So it is with us, exiles on Earth and sojourners longing for our permanent home. In the meantime, the nations are here "and they shall be called The Holy People, The Redeemed of the Lord; and you shall be called Sought Out, A City Not Forsaken" (Isaiah 62:12).

APPENDIX A

WORLDVIEW IDENTIFICATION WORKBOOK

This workbook is designed to be photocopied and taken into the community when conducting ethnographic research. Chapter 6 provides an explanation of how to carry out the research and should be read first.

The next page contains a simple chart that can be used to gather basic demographic information about people in the community. This chart can be used when only brief encounters are expected. If time and relationship permits, use the second survey which can take 1 – 2 hours to administer but provides much more detail on the worldview and cultural identity of people living in your community. We recommend at least memorizing the five Fs and using them to frame conversations. If time and circumstances permit, use the workbook and ask the listed questions. These questions are designed to gather information on a wide range of topics and will help form the basis of understanding the culture and contextualizing the church.

These questions are only meant to be a guide and feel free to leave some out or add your own as the context permits. You will hopefully find the survey a fun activity and a helpful bridge to talking about spiritual issues and sharing the gospel.

Basic Demographic Survey

Date:
Location/Neighborhood:
Thank you for meeting with me to help me learn more about your culture. I'd like to start by asking a few questions about your people here in the United States.

Where are you from?

How long have you lived here?

What do you call people from your culture?

How many of your people live in the city? What areas do they live in?

What language do you speak at home?

What is the primary religion of your people? Are their nearby places of worship?

Do you know of any local print or web news resources for your people or in your language?

What are some essential needs in your community?

Family

I'd like to ask you a few questions about your family. Is that ok?
What does your household look like, who lives with you?

What language do you speak at home?

Can you marry outside of your culture?

What does a wedding look like?

Who makes the major decisions in the household?

What responsibilities do children have related to the family?
Does the eldest have any specific responsibilities?

Do your ancestors have any present role in your family? How so?

Friends

I'd like to ask you a few questions about your friends here in the U.S. Is that ok?

What is it like living here? Are there many people from your culture?

In what parts of town do most people from your culture live?

What kinds of jobs do they have?

Where do you spend time with friends and what do you like to do?

What has been your experience with Americans?

How are friendships different here that those in your home culture?

Food

I'd like to talk about your favorite foods. Is that ok?
What are your favorite foods?

What do you think of American food?

Does your culture have a famous dish?

Are their drinks, foods, or animals you avoid eating? Why?

What special meals do you have at religious events?

Does your culture have guidelines for who prepares the food, how it is served, or in what order family members eat?

Festivals
May I ask a few questions about holidays and festivals in your culture?
What religion is most common in your culture? Do you practice that religion?

Are their special days of the year or major festivals or holidays you observe?

What is the significance of each one?

Are the festivals different here than in your home country? How so?

Could I attend one of your festivals sometime?

Have you heard of Jesus? What do you know about him?

Future
Lastly, may I ask a few questions about what you think about the future?
What happens after someone dies in your culture?

How do you best prepare for death and beyond?

How do you relate to your ancestors who have gone to the afterlife?

Do they still influence your life? How so?

How do you relate to god/creator?

Are time and history moving forward or are they cyclical or circular?

What are you most excited about the future?

What are the biggest challenges and needs facing your people here?

APPENDIX B

ORALITY SURVEY TOOL

By Lynne L. Abney (based on Walter Ong, *Orality & Literacy*) Each set of statements, left and right, describes the ends of 40 communication style "poles." You may administer the survey yourself, or leave it with someone to complete on their own. Ask them to think specifically about each situation, and circle the number that best represents his or her behavior in each learning situation. (Example: For #1, if you were evaluating yourself and "have to see the word written down to remember it," you would circle 3 or 4). Follow the directions at the end to score the assessment. The results help you know how to communicate truth most clearly to a listener with that learning preference.

Basic learning preferences: My friend's name is: _____ ORAL COMMUNICATORS	scale	PRINT COMMUNICATORS
...learn by hearing ("I'm an aural learner.")	0 1 2 3 4	...learn by seeing ("I'm a visual learner.")
...learn by observing and imitating, by listening and repeating, by memorizing proverbs, traditional sayings, stories, songs, and expressions.	0 1 2 3 4	...learn by reading non-fiction, by studying, examining, classifying, comparing, analyzing.
...think and talk about events, not words. (Words function to paint action pictures.)	0 1 2 3 4	...think and talk about words, concepts, and principles. (Words are perceived as representing objects more than actions.)
...use stories of human action to store, organize, and communicate much of what they know"; information is "embedded in the flow of time" usually on a "story line".	0 1 2 3 4	... manage knowledge "in elaborate, more or less scientifically abstract categories", and store it in print rather than in stories.
...value and learn information handed down from the past.	0 1 2 3 4	...seek to discover new information.
...value traditional solutions.	0 1 2 3 4	...value innovative solutions.
SUBTOTAL 1		**BASIC LEARNING**

Importance of sound: ORAL COMMUNICATORS	scale	PRINT COMMUNICATORS
...are deeply affected by the sound of what they hear.	0 1 2 3 4	...are affected by the content of what they read.
...prize clarity and style of speech.	0 1 2 3 4	...prize clarity and validity of reasoning.
...view speech primarily as a way of relating to people, or as a form of entertainment.	0 1 2 3 4	...view speech primarily as a means of conveying information.
...respond to a speaker while he is speaking and participate in the story telling.	0 1 2 3 4	...generally read or listen quietly.
...engage in verbal contests, trying to excel in praise, insults, riddles, jokes, etc.	0 1 2 3 4	...engage in few verbal contests, but write letters to the editor, etc.
...believe that oral exchange should normally be formal, carefully articulated.	0 1 2 3 4	...believe that oral exchange should normally be informal, casual.
...can produce, in some cases, beautiful verbal art forms, such as poetry and ballads.	0 1 2 3 4	...can produce, in some cases, interesting literature, but generally not verbal art forms of a high quality.
...view a written text as a record of something spoken or an aid to memorization or recitation.	0 1 2 3 4	...view a written text as a vessel of information.
...prefer to read aloud or at least imagine the sounds of the words as they read.	0 1 2 3 4	...prefer to read alone, taking in the content of the words but not their sound.
SUBTOTAL 2	SOUND	

Importance of real-life experience: ORAL COMMUNICATORS	scale	PRINT COMMUNICATORS
…learn and retain knowledge in relation to real or imagined events in human life.	0 1 2 3 4	…learn and retain knowledge as general principles, with events as examples.
…may recite genealogies but make few lists.	0 1 2 3 4	…make lists but recite few genealogies.
…relate closely and personally to the people and events they know about.	0 1 2 3 4	…relate more objectively to what they know, because writing comes between them.
…think and talk mostly about events and people.	0 1 2 3 4	…think and write about their own feelings and thoughts as well.
…reason from experience and association.	0 1 2 3 4	…reason by means of "formal" logic, using analysis and explanation.
…organize non-narrative speeches (such as exhortations and sermons) largely by recounting events associated with the point being made or with the words being used.	0 1 2 3 4	…organize non-narrative speeches (such as exhortations and sermons) by laying out a logical progression of thoughts.
SUBTOTAL 3	REAL-LIFE EXPERIENCE	

Style preference: ORAL COMMUNICATORS	scale	PRINT COMMUNICATORS
…communicate by joining sentences with conjunctions such as 'and', 'then'.	0 1 2 3 4	…communicate by joining sentences with subjunctives such as 'while', 'after'.
…can organize experiences and episodes.	0 1 2 3 4	…can organize long, logical arguments.
…construct longer narratives by stringing episodes together; themes may be repeated in several episodes.	0 1 2 3 4	…construct narratives with chronologically linear plots that reach a climax and resolution; any themes are validated by the outcome.
…use symbols and stories to carry the message.	0 1 2 3 4	…use charts, diagrams, and lists to explain the message.
…frequently use words in set phrases, such as sayings, proverbs, riddles, formulas, or just descriptions such as 'brave soldier'.	0 1 2 3 4	…generally use words independently, with few set phrases.
…appreciate repetition, in case something was missed the first time.	0 1 2 3 4	…do not like repetition, since material missed can be read again.
…like verbosity (many words to say a little)	0 1 2 3 4	…like brevity (few words to say much)
SUBTOTAL 4	STYLE	

Importance of dialogue: ORAL COMMUNICATORS	scale	PRINT COMMUNICATORS
...tend to communicate in groups.	0 1 2 3 4	...tend to communicate one-to-one.
...learn mostly in interaction with other people.	0 1 2 3 4	...learn mostly alone.
...cannot think about something very long without dialogue.	0 1 2 3 4	...can think about something for a long time while making notes about it, etc.

SUBTOTAL 5	DIALOGUE

Importance of drama and melodrama: ORAL COMMUNICATORS	scale	PRINT COMMUNICATORS
...employ exaggerated praise and scorn.	0 1 2 3 4	...intentionally moderate their praise and scorn.
...drawn "heavy" characters in their stories.	0 1 2 3 4	...prefer realistic characters in stories.
...create art forms that emphasize struggle against an enemy.	0 1 2 3 4	...create art forms that emphasize struggle to reach a goal or overcome an obstacle.
...use their hands to help express themselves when they tell stories, through gestures or by playing musical instruments.	0 1 2 3 4	...use their hands little, since gestures are not written or read.

SUBTOTAL 6	DRAMA AND MELODRAMA

Importance of context: ORAL COMMUNICATORS	scale	PRINT COMMUNICATORS
...view matters in the totality of their context, including everyone involved (holistically)	0 1 2 3 4	...view matters abstractly and analytically (compartmentally).
...leave much of the message unverbalized, depending instead on shared situation, shared culture, intonation, facial gestures, and hand gestures to help communicate the message.	0 1 2 3 4	...clarify the message by using words rather than context, gesture, or intonation which cannot be conveyed in print.
...can be imprecise, and clarify as needed, based on the listener's reaction.	0 1 2 3 4	...learn to avoid ambiguity because it cannot be clarified by an author at a distance.
...avoid asking or answering "direct" questions.	0 1 2 3 4	...ask and answer "direct" questions.
...are uninterested in definitions since the context renders them superfluous.	0 1 2 3 4	...appreciate definitions.
SUBTOTAL 7	CONTEXT	

Add the circled numbers in each set of choices. Write the subtotals below and add them together. *Be sure you answered all the questions, even if you had to guess or didn't really know.*

BASIC LEARNING

TOTAL _____
LOCATE THIS SCORE
ON THE **ORALITY**
SCALE BELOW

SUBTOTAL 1 _____
SUBTOTAL 2 _____   SOUND
SUBTOTAL 3 _____   LIFE EXPERIENCE
SUBTOTAL 4 _____   STYLE
SUBTOTAL 5 _____   DIALOGUE
SUBTOTAL 6 _____   DRAMA AND
                         MELODRAMA
SUBTOTAL 7 _____   CONTEXT

BIBLIOGRAPHY

Books

Addison, Steve. *Movements that Change the World: Five Keys to Spreading the Gospel*. Downers Grove, IL: InterVarsity Press, 2011.

Alasuutari, Pertti. *Researching Culture: Qualitative Method and Cultural Studies*. Thousand Oaks, CA: SAGE Publications, 1996.

Alba, Richard, and Victor Nee. *Remaking the American Mainstream: Assimilation and Contemporary Immigration*. Cambridge, MA: Harvard University Press, 2003.

Allen, Roland. *Missionary Methods: St. Paul's or Ours?* Grand Rapids: William B. Eerdmans Publishing Company, 1997.

_____. *The Spontaneous Expansion of the Church and the Causes Which Hinder It*. London: World Dominion Press, 1949.

Amit, Vered, ed. *Realizing Community: Concepts, Social Relationships and Sentiments*. London: Routledge, 2002.

Anderson, E. *Streetwise: Race, Class and Change in an Urban Community*. Chicago: University of Chicago Press, 1990.

Anderson, Rufus. "Principles and Methods of Modern Missions." In *To Advance the Gospel: Selections from the Writings of Rufus Anderson*, ed., R. Pierce Beaver, 97-102. Grand Rapids: William B. Eerdmans Publishing Company, 1967.

Angrosino, Michael. *Projects in Ethnographic Research*. Long Grove, IL: Waveland Press, 2005.

Armstrong, Hayward, ed. *Tell the Story: A Primer on Chronological Bible Storying*. Rockville, VA: International Centre for Excellence in Leadership, 2003.

Ashford, Bruce Riley. *Theology and Practice of Mission: God, the Church, and the Nations*. Nashville: B & H Academic, 2011.

Baker, Susan S., ed. *Globalization and Its Effects on Urban Ministry in the 21ˢᵗ Century*. Pasadena, CA: William Carey Library, 2009.

Barton, David, Mary Hamilton, and Roz Ivanic. Eds. *Situated Literacies: Reading and Writing in Context*. London: Routledge, 1999.

Bennett, Shane, and Kim Felder. *Exploring the Land: Discovering Ways for Unreached People to Follow Christ*. Littleton, CO: Caleb Project, 2003.

Bernard, H. Russell. *Research Methods in Anthropology: Qualitative and Quantitative Methods*. 3ʳᵈ ed. Walnut Creek, CA: Alta Mira Press, 2002.

Bierstedt, Robert. *The Social Order*. 3ʳᵈ ed. New York: McGraw Hill, 1970.

Boomershine, Thomas B. *Story Journey: An Invitation to the Gospel as Storytelling*. Nashville: Abingdon Press, 1988.

Boshart, David W. *Becoming Missional: Denominations and New Church Development in Complex Social Contexts*. Eugene, OR: Wipf & Stock, 2011.

Braziel, Jana Evans, and Anita Mannur, eds. *Theorizing Diaspora: A Reader*. Malden, MA: Blackwell Publishing, 2003.

Brock, Charles. *The Principles and Practice of Indigenous Church Planting*. Nashville: Broadman Press, 1981.

Carlton, R. Bruce. *Amazing Grace: Lessons on Church Planting Movements from Cambodia*. Chennai, India: Mission Educational Books, 2000.

_____. *Strategy Coordinator: Changing the Course of Southern Baptist Missions*. Eugene, OR: Wipf & Stock, 2011.

Chaney, Charles L. *Church Planting at the End of the Twentieth Century*. Wheaton, IL: Tyndale House Publishers, 1982.

Chester, Tim, and Steve Timmis. *Total Church: A Radical Reshaping around Gospel and Community*. Wheaton, IL: Crossway, 2008.

Collins, James, and Richard Blot. *Literacy and Literacies: Texts, Power and Identity*. New York: Cambridge University Press, 2002.

Conn, Harvie M. *The American City and the Evangelical Church: A Historical Overview*. Grand Rapids: Baker House, 1994.

134

_____. *A Clarified Vision for Urban Mission*. Grand Rapids: Zondervan, 1987.

_____. *Eternal Word and Changing Worlds: Theology, Anthropology and Mission in Trialogue*. Grand Rapids: Zondervan, 1984.

_____. *Evangelism: Doing Justice and Preaching Grace*. Grand Rapids: Academie Books, 1982.

_____. *Planting and Growing Urban Churches: From Dream to Reality*. Wake Forest, NC: Baker House, 1997.

Conn, Harvie M., and Manuel Ortiz. *Urban Ministry: The Kingdom, the City, and the People of God*. Downers Grove, IL: InterVarsity Press, 2001.

Creswell, John. *Qualitative Inquiry and Research Design: Choosing Among Five Traditions*. Thousand Oaks, CA: SAGE Publications, 1998.

Cupit, Tony. *Five till Midnight: Church Planting for A.D. 2000 and Beyond*. Atlanta: Home Mission Board of the Southern Baptist Conventions, 1994.

Dewey, Joanna. "The Gospel of Mark as an Oral-Aural Event: Implications for Interpretation." In *New Literary Criticism and the New Testament*, ed. Elizabeth Struthers Malbon and Edgar V. McKnight. Sheffield, England: Sheffield Academic Press, 1994.

DeYmaz, Mark. *Building a Healthy Multi-ethnic Church: Mandate, Commitments, and Practices of a Diverse Congregation*. San Francisco: Jossey-Bass, 2007.

DeYoung, Kevin, and Greg Gilbert. *What is the Mission of the Church: Making Sense of Social Justice, Shalom, and the Great Commission*. Wheaton, IL: Crossway, 2011.

Do, Hien Doc. *The Vietnamese Americans: The New Americans*. Westport, CT: Greenwood Press, 1999.

Driscoll, Mark, and Gary Breshears. *Vintage Church: Timeless Truths and Timely Methods*. Wheaton, IL: Crossway, 2008.

Eames, Edwin, and Judith Goode. *Anthropology of the City: An Introduction to Urban Anthropology*. Englewood Cliffs, NJ: Prentice-Hall, Inc., 1977.

Edwards, Jonathan, ed. *The Life and Diary of David Brainerd*. Grand Rapids: Baker Book House, 2005.

Engel, James F. *How Can I Get Them to Listen?* Grand Rapids: Zondervan, 1977.

Etherington, Norman, ed. *Missions and Empire*. Oxford: Oxford University Press, 2007.

Ferguson, Dave. *Exponential: How You and Your Friends can Start a Missional Church Movement*. Grand Rapids: Zondervan, 2010.

Fetterman, David M. *Ethnography:Step-by-Step*. 3rd ed. Thousand Oaks, CA: Sage Publications, 2009.

Fisher, Claude. *The Urban Experience*. 2nd ed. San Diego, CA: Harcourt Brace Jovanovich, 1984.

Fishman, Joshua. *The Sociology of Language*. Rowley, MA: Newbury, 1972.

Fishman, Sylvia Barack. *Jewish and Something Else: A Study of Mixed-Married Families*. New York: American Jewish Committee, 2001.

Foner, Nancy, and Ruben Rumbaut, eds. *Immigration Research for a New Century*. New York: Russell Sage Foundation, 2000.

Francis, Hozell C. *Church Planting in the African-American Context: Shape a Vision, Plan Wisely, Know your Community, Lead Effectively, Reach Families, Transcend Ethnic Boundaries*. Grand Rapids: Zondervan, 1999.

Fuder, John, ed. *A Heart for the City: Effective Ministries to the Urban Community*. Chicago: Moody Press, 1999.

Fuder, John, and Noel Castellanos, eds. *A Heart for the Community: New Models for Urban and Suburban Ministry*. Chicago: Moody Publishers, 2009.

Fujino, Gary, Timothy Sisk, and Tereso Casino, eds. *Reaching the City: Reflections on Urban Mission for the Twenty-first Century*. Pasadena, CA: Evangelical Missiological Society, 2012.

Galloway, Bryan. *Traveling Down Their Road: A Workbook for Discovering a People's Worldview*. Self Published, 2006.

Garrison, David. *Church Planting Movements: How God is Redeeming a Lost World*. Midlothian, VA: WIGTake Resources, 2004.

Gibson, Margaret. *Accommodation without Assimilation: Sikh Immigrants in an American High School*. Ithaca, NY: Cornell University Press, 1988.

Goody, Jack. *The Domestication of the Savage Mind*. Cambridge: Cambridge University Press, 1977.

_____. *The Interface between the Written and the Oral*. Cambridge: Cambridge University Press, 1987.

Goody, Jack, and Ian Watt. "The Consequences of Literacy" in *Literacy in Traditional Societies*. Edited by Jack Goody. Cambridge: Cambridge University Press, 1968.

Gordon, Milton. *Assimilation in American Life*. New York: Oxford University Press, 1964.

Gottidiener, Mark, and Leslie Budd, eds. *Key Concepts in Urban Studies*. London: SAGE Publications, 2006.

Graham, William A. *Beyond the Written Word: Oral Aspects of Scripture in the History of Religion*. Cambridge: Cambridge University Press, 1987.

Grigg, Viv. *Cry of the Urban Poor*. Monrovia, CA: MARC, 1992.

Greenway, Roger S. *Discipling the City: A Comprehensive Approach to Urban Mission*. 2nd Ed. Grand Rapids: Baker Book House, 1992.

_____. *Guidelines for Urban Church Planting*. Grand Rapids: Baker Book House, 1976.

Greenway, Roger S., and Harvie M. Conn. *Discipling the City: Theological Reflections on Urban Mission*. Grand Rapids: Baker Book House, 1979.

Greenway, Roger, and Timothy Monsma. *Cities: Missions' New Frontier*. 2nd edition. Grand Rapids: Baker Books, 2000.

Gupta, Paul R. *Breaking Tradition to Accomplish Vision: Training Leaders for a Church-Planting Movement*. Winona Lake, IN: BMH Books, 2006.

Hall, Edward T. *The Hidden Dimension*. Garden City, NY: Doubleday & Company, 1966.

Hammond, Scott, and Dan Peterson. "Orality." In *Encyclopedia of Religion, Communication, and Media*, ed. Daniel Stout. New York: Routledge, 2006.

Hannerz, Ulf. *Exploring the City*. New York: Columbia University Press, 1980.

Harris, Richard H. *Reaching a Nation through Church Planting*. Alpharetta, GA: North American Mission Board, SBC, 2002.

Havelock, Eric. *Preface to Plato*. Cambridge, MA: Harvard University Press, 1963.

Healey, Joseph. *Towards an African Narrative Theology*. Maryknoll, NY: Orbis Books, 1996.

Hesselgrave, David J. *Communicating Christ Cross-Culturally*. 2nd ed. Grand Rapids: Zondervan, 1991.

_____. *Planting Churches Cross-Culturally: North America and Beyond*. 2nd ed. Grand Rapids: Baker Academic, 2000.

Hesselgrave, David J., and Edward Rommen. *Contextualization: Meanings, Methods, and Models*. Pasadena: William Carey Library, 2003.

Hesselgrave, David, and Ed Stetzer. *Missionshift: Global Mission Issues in the Third Millennium*. Nashville: B & H Academic, 2010.

Hiebert, Paul G. *Anthropological Insights for Missionaries*. Grand Rapids: Baker Academic, 1986.

_____. *Anthropological Reflections on Missiological Issues*. Grand Rapids: Baker Academic, 1994.

_____. *The Gospel in Human Contexts: Anthropological Explorations for Contemporary Missions*. Grand Rapids: Baker Academic, 2009.

_____. *Transforming Worldviews: An Anthropological Understanding of How People Change*. Grand Rapids: Baker Academic, 2008.

Hiebert, Paul G., and Eloise Hiebert Menneses. *Incarnational Ministry: Planting Churches in Band, Tribal, Peasant, and Urban Societies*. Grand Rapids: Baker House, 1995.

Hipps, Shane A. *The Hidden Power of Electronic Culture: How Media Shapes Faith, the Gospel, and Church*. Grand Rapids: Zondervan, 2005.

Hunt, E. B. *Concept Learning*. New York: Wiley Press, 1962.

Jackson, J. David, ed. *PlantLife: Principles and Practices in Church Planting.* Smyrna, DE: Missional Press, 2008.

Jansen, Frank K. *Target Earth: The Necessity of Diversity in a Holistic Perspective on World Mission.* Kailua-Kona, HI: University of the Nations, 1989.

Jenkins, Philip. *The Next Christendom: The Coming of Global Christianity* (New York: Oxford University Press, 2007.

Johnson, Dennis, and Joe Musser. *Tell Me a Story: Orality-How the World Learns.* Colorado Springs: David C. Cook, 2012.

Jones, Tom. *Church Planting from the Ground Up.* Joplin, MO: College Press Publishing Co., 2004.

Kasinitz, Philip. *Caribbean New York: Black Immigrants and the Politics of Race.* Ithaca, NY: Cornell University Press, 1992.

Kennedy School of Government. *Immigration in America: The NPR/Kaiser/Kennedy School Immigration Survey.* Cambridge, MA: Harvard University, John F. Kennedy School of Government, 2009.

Klem, Herbert V. *Oral Communication of the Scripture: Insights from African Oral Art.* Pasadena, CA: William Carey Library, 1982.

Koh, Jaime, and Stephanie Ho. *Culture and Customs of Singapore and Malaysia.* Santa Barbara: Greenwood Press, 2009.

Kozinets, Robert V. *Netnography: Doing Ethnographic Research Online.* Thousand Oaks, CA: SAGE, 2010.

Kraft, Charles. *Anthropology for Christian Witness.* Maryknoll, NY: Orbis Books, 1996.

Kirtz, Mary, Charles Keely, and Sylvano Tomasi, eds. *Global Trends in Migration.* Staten Island, NY: CMS Press, 1981.

Kugelmass, Jack. *The Greenwich Village Halloween Parade.* New York: Columbia University Press, 1994.

Kwong, Peter. *Chinatown, New York: Labour and Politics, 1930-1950.* New York: Monthly Review Press, 1979.

_____. *The New Chinatown.* New York: Hill and Wong, 1996.

Larson, Joanne, and Jackie Marsh. *Making Literacy Real: Theories and Practices for Learning and Teaching*. Thousand Oaks, CA: Sage Publications, 2005.

Lawless, Charles E., and Thom S. Rainer. Editors. *The Challenge of The Great Commission: Essays on God's Mandate for the Local Church*. Crestwood, KY: Pinnacle Publishers, 2005.

Le Compte, Margaret, and Jean Schensul. *Ethnographer's Toolkit*. 7 vols. Lanham, MD: Alta Mira Press, 1999.

Lederer, William J., and Eugene Burdick. *The Ugly American*. New York: W. W. Norton and Company, 1958.

Lévi-Strauss, Claude. *The Savage Mind*. Chicago: University of Chicago Press, 1966.

Lewis, Larry. *The Church Planter's Handbook*. Nashville: Broadman Press, 1992.

Lewis, Richard. *The Cultural Imperative: Global Trends in the 21st Century*. Boston: Intercultural Press, 2007.

Loughlin, Gerard. *Telling God's Story: Bible, Church, and Narrative Theology*. Cambridge: Cambridge University Press, 1996.

Lord, Albert. *The Singer of Tales*. Cambridge, MA: Harvard University Press, 1964.

Low, Setha, ed. *Theorizing the City: The New Urban Anthropology Reader*. New Brunswick, NJ: Rutgers University Press, 1999.

Luria, Aleksandr. *Cognitive Development: Its Cultural and Social Foundations*. Edited by Michael Cole. Translated by Martin Lopez-Morillas and Lynn Solotaroff. Cambridge, MA: Harvard University Press, 1976.

Luso-American Development Foundation, ed. *Metropolis International Workshop Proceedings*. Lisbon, Portugal: Fundacao Luso-American para o Desenvolvimento, 1998.

Maffesoli, Michel. *The Time of the Tribes: The Decline of Individualism in Mass Society*. Translated by Don Smith. London: SAGE Publications, 1996.

Malinowski, Bronislaw. "The Problem of Meaning in Primitive Languages." In *The Meaning of Meaning*, ed. C. K. Ogden and Ivor Richards. London: K. Paul, Trench, Trubner & Co., 1936.

_____. *Myth in Primitive Psychology*. London: Kegan Paul, Trench, Trubner and Company, 1926.

Malphurs, Aubrey. *Planting Growing Churches for the 21st Century: A Comprehensive Guide for New Churches and Those Desiring Renewal*. 2nd ed. Grand Rapids: Baker Books, 1998.

_____. *The Nuts and Bolts of Church Planting: A Guide for Starting Any Kind of Church*. Grand Rapids: Baker Books, 2011.

Mangin, William, ed. *Peasants in Cities: Readings in the Anthropology of Urbanization*. Boston: Houghton Mifflin Company, 1970.

Mannoia, Kevin W. *Church Planting: The Next Generation: Introducing the Century 21 Church Planting System*. Indianapolis, IN: Light and Life Press, 1996.

Massey, Douglas, and Magaly Sanchez. *Brokered Boundaries: Creating Immigrant Identity in Anti-Immigrant Times*. New York: Russell Sage Foundation, 2010.

Marris, P. *Family and Social Change in an African City: A Study of Rehousing in Lagos*. Evanston, IL: Northwestern University Press, 1962.

McCurdy, David W., James P. Spradley, and Dianna J. Shandy. *The Cultural Experience: Ethnography in Complex Society*. 2nd ed. Long Grove, IL: Waveland Press, 2004.

McGavran, Donald Anderson. *Crucial Issues in Missions Tomorrow*. Chicago: Moody Press, 1972.

McKinley, Mike. *Church Planting is for Wimps: How God Uses Messed-Up People to Plant Ordinary Churches that do Extraordinary Things*. Wheaton, IL: Crossway, 2010.

McKinney, Carol. *Globe-Trotting in Sandals: A Field Guide to Cultural Research*. Dallas: SIL International, 2000.

McNamara, Roger N. *The Y-B-H Handbook of Church Planting: A Practical Guide to Church Planting*. Longwood, FL: Xulon Press, 2005.

Moreau, A. Scott, David Burnett, Harold Netland, and Charles Edward Van Engen. *Evangelical Dictionary of World Missions*. Grand Rapids: Baker Books, 2000.

Mullings, Leith, ed. *Cities of the United States: Studies in Urban Anthropology*. New York: Columbia University Press, 1987.

Neighbour, Ralph Webster. *Planting Urban Churches in Non-Christian Contexts*. Tacoma, WA: Evangelical Theological Society, 1989.

_____. *Where do We go from Here? A Guidebook for Cell Group Churches*. Houston: Touch Publications, 1990.

Neill, Stephen. *A History of Christian Missions*, 2nd ed. London: Penguin Group, 1990.

Nehrbass, Kenneth. *Christianity and Animism in Melanesia: Four Approaches to Gospel and Culture*. Pasadena, CA: William Carey Library, 2012.

Nevius, John L. *The Planting and Development of Missionary Churches*. Hancock, NH: Monadnock Press, 2003, originally published in 1886.

Nichols, Laurie Fortunak, A. Scott Moreau, and Gary Corwin. *Extending God's Kingdom: Church Planting Yesterday, Today, and Tomorrow*. Wheaton, IL: Evangelism and Missions Information Service, 2011.

Nida, Eugene Albert. *Customs and Cultures: Anthropology for Christian Missions*. New York: Harper, 1954.

_____. *God's Word in Man's Language*. New York: Harper, 1952.

_____. *Language Structure and Translation: Essays*. Stanford, CA: Stanford University Press, 1975.

_____. *Message and Mission: The Communication of the Christian Faith*. New York: Harper, 1960.

North American Mission Board, *Bivocational Church Planters: Uniquely Wired for Kingdom Growth*. Alpharetta, GA: North American Mission Board, SBS, 2008.

O'Connor, John Patrick. *Reproducible Pastoral Training: Church-Planting Guidelines from the Teachings of George Patterson*. Pasadena: William Carey Library, 2006.

142

OECD. *Redefining "Urban": A New Way to Measure Metropolitan Areas*. n.p.: OECD Publishing, 2012. http://dx.doi.org/10.1787 /9789264174108-en. Accessed August 31, 2012.

Olson, Bruce. *Bruchko*. Lake Mary, FL: Charisma House, 1995.

Ong, Walter J. *Interfaces of the Word: Studies in the Evolution of Consciousness and Culture*. Ithaca, NY: Cornell University Press, 1977.

_____. *Orality and Literacy: The Technologizing of the Word*. New York: Methuen, 1982.

_____. *The Presence of the Word: Some Prolegomena for Cultural and Religious History*. New York: Simon and Schuster, 1970.

Ott, Craig. *Global Church Planting: Biblical Principles and Best Practices for Multiplication*. Grand Rapids: Baker Academic, 2011.

Ott, Craig, and Harold Netland, eds. *Globalizing Theology: Belief and Practice in an Era of World Christianity*. Grand Rapids: Baker Academic, 2006.

Park, Robert and Ernest Burgess. *The City*. Chicago: University of Chicago Press, 1974.

Parry, Milman. *The Making of Homeric Verse*. Edited by Adam Parry. Oxford: Clarendon Press, 1971.

Patrick, Darrin. *Church Planter: The Man, the Message, the Mission*. Wheaton: Crossway Publishers, 2010.

Payne, J. D. *The Barnabas Factors: Eight Essential Practices of Church Planting Team Members*. Smyrna, DE: Missional Press, 2008.

_____. *Discovering Church Planting: An Introduction to the Whats, Whys, and Hows of Global Church Planting*. Colorado Springs: Paternoster, 2009.

Missional House Churches: Reaching our Communities with the Gospel. Colorado Springs: Paternoster Publishing, 2008.

_____. *Strangers Next Door: Immigration, Migration and Mission*. Downers Grove, IL: InterVaristy Press, 2012.

Perry, Robert L. *Models of Multi-Family Housing Ministry*. Atlanta: Home Mission Board, SBC, 1989.

Pocock, Michael, Gailyn Van Rheenen, and Douglas McConnell. *The Changing Face of World Missions: Engaging Contemporary Issues and Trends.* Grand Rapids: Baker Books, 2005.

Portes, Alejandro, ed. *The Economic Sociology of Immigration: Essays on Networks, Ethnicity and Entrepreneurship.* New York: Russell Sage Foundation, 1995.

Portes, Alejandro, and Robert Bach. *Latin Journey: Cuban and Mexican Immigrants in the U.S.* Berkeley, CA: University of California Press, 1985.

Price, Marie, and Lisa Benton-Short. Editors. *Migrants to the Metropolis: The Rise of Immigrant Gateway Cites.* Syracuse, NY: Syracuse University Press, 2008.

Ratliff, Joe S. *Church Planting in the African-American Community.* Nashville: Broadman Press, 1993.

Register, Ray G. *Back to Jerusalem: Church Planting Movements in the Holy Land.* Enumclaw, WA: WinePress, 2000.

Robinson, Martin. *Planting Mission-Shaped Churches Today.* Grand Rapids: Monarch Books, 2006.

Romo, Oscar I. *American Mosaic: Church Planting in Ethnic America.* Nashville: Broadman Press, 1993.

Rowland, Trent. *Pioneer Church Planting: A Rookie Team Leader's Handbook.* Littleton, CO: Caleb Project, 2001.

Rubin, Herbert, and Irene Rubin. *Qualitative Interviewing: The Art of Hearing Data.* Thousand Oaks, CA: SAGE Publications, 1995.

Ruble, Blair, Lisa Hanley, and Allison Garland, eds. *Immigration and Integration in Urban Communities: Renegotiating the City.* Washington, DC: Woodrow Wilson Center Press, 2008.

Rynkiewich, Michael. *Soul, Self, and Society: A Postmodern Anthropology for Mission in a Postcolonial World.* Eugene, OR: Cascade Books, 2011.

Sample, Tex. *Blue-Collar Ministry: Facing Economic and Social Realities of Working People.* Valley Forge, PA: Judson Press, 1984.

_____. *Hard Living People & Mainstream Christians.* Nashville: Abingdon Press, 1993.

_____. *Ministry in an Oral Culture: Living with Will Rogers, Uncle Remus, and Minnie Pearl*. Louisville: John Knox Press, 1994.

_____. *The Spectacle of Worship in a Wired World: Electronic Culture and the Gathered People of God*. Nashville: Abingdon Press, 1998.

Schensul, Jean J., and Margaret Diane LeCompte *Analyzing & Interpreting Ethnographic Data*. Vol. 5. Walnut Creek, CA: AltaMira Press, 1999.

_____. *Designing & Conducting Ethnographic Research*. Vol. 1. Walnut Creek, CA: AltaMira Press, 1999.

Searcy, Nelson. *Launch: Starting a New Church from Scratch*. Ventura, CA: Regal Books, 2006.

Sheard, Daniel. *An Orality Primer for Missionaries*. n.p., 2007.

Shenk, David W. *Creating Communities of the Kingdom: New Testament Models of Church Planting*. Scottdale, PA: Herald Press, 1988.

Sills, M. David. *Reaching and Teaching: A Call to Great Commission Obedience*. Chicago: Moody Publishers, 2010.

Sinclair, Daniel. *A Vision of the Possible: Pioneer Church Planting in Teams*. Downers Grove, IL: IVP Press, 2006.

Southern Baptist Convention. *Ethnic Church Planting Guide*. Atlanta, GA: The Home Mission Board, 1993.

Guide for Establishing New Churches and Missions: Evangelizing and Congregationalizing. Atlanta: The Home Mission Board, 1978.

_____. *Reaching Hispanics in North America: Helping you Understand and Engage One of God's Greatest Mission Fields*. Alpharetta, GA: The North American Mission Board, 2009.

_____. *Stimulating and Nurturing Church Planting Movements*. Rockville, VA: International Centre for Excellence in Leadership, International Mission Board, SBC, 2001.

Sowell, Thomas. *Ethnic America: A History*. New York: Basic Books, 1981.

Spradley, James P. *The Ethnographic Interview*. New York: Holt, Rinehart, and Winston, 1979.

_____. *Participant Observation*. New York: Holt, Rinehart and Winston, 1980.

Steffen Tom A. *Encountering Missionary Life and Work: Preparing for Intercultural Ministry*. Grand Rapids: Baker Academic, 2008.

_____. *The Facilitator Era: Beyond Pioneer Church Multiplication*. Eugene, OR: WIPF & Stock, 2011.

_____. *Passing the Baton: Church Planting that Empowers*. La Habra, CA: Center for Organizational and Ministry Development, 1997.

_____. *Planned Phase-Out: A Checklist for Cross-Cultural Church Planters*. San Francisco: Austin & Winfield, 1992.

_____. *Reconnecting God's Story to Ministry: Cross-Cultural Storytelling at Home and Abroad*. Rev. Ed. Waynesboro, GA: Authentic Media, 2005.

Stetzer, Ed. *Breaking the Missional Code: Your Church can Become a Missionary in your Community*. Nashville: Broadman & Holman, 2006.

_____. *Planting Missional Churches*. Nashville: Broadman & Holman, 2006.

_____. *Planting New Churches in a Postmodern Age*. Nashville: Broadman & Holman, 2003.

_____. *Viral Churches: Helping Church Planters Become Movement Makers*. San Francisco: Jossey-Bass, 2010.

Strauss, Anselm, and Juliet Corbin. *Basics of Qualitative Research: Techniques and Procedures for Developing Grounded Theory*, 2nd ed. Thousand Oaks, CA: SAGE Publications, 1998.

Street, Brian, ed. *Cross-Cultural Approaches to Literacy*. Cambridge: Cambridge University Press, 1993.

_____, ed. *Literacy and Development: Ethnographic Perspectives*. London: New York: Routledge, 2001.

_____. *Literacy in Theory and Practice*. Cambridge, UK: Cambridge University Press, 1984.

_____. *Social Literacies: Critical Approaches to Literacy in Education, Development and Ethnography*. London: Longman, 1995.

Susser, Ida. *Norman Street*. New York: Oxford University Press, 1982.

Susser, Ida, and Thomas Patterson, eds. *Cultural Diversity in the United States: A Critical Reader*. Malden, MA: Blackwell Publishers, 2001.

Sutter, Kevin. *Keys to Church Planting Movements: The Adventures of Stephanas, First Century Disciple*. McKinleyville, CA: Asteroidea Books, 2006.

Tennent, Timothy. *Theology in the Context of World Christianity: How the Global Church in Influencing the Way we Think about and Discuss Theology*. Grand Rapids: Zondervan, 2007.

Tippett, Alan. *Verdict Theology in Mission Theory*. Lincoln, IL: Lincoln Christian College Press, 1969.

Towns, Elmer L. *Churches that Multiply: A Bible Study on Church Planting*. Kansas City, MO: Beacon Hill Press of Kansas City, 2003.

Rucker, Ruth. *From Jerusalem to Irian Jaya*. Grand Rapids: Zondervan, 1983.

United States Department of Homeland Security. *Yearbook of Immigration Statistics: 2009*. Washington, DC: U.S. Department of Homeland Security, Office of Immigration Statistics, 2010.

Van Engen, Charles Edward. *God's Missionary People: Rethinking the Purpose of the Local Church*. Grand Rapids: Baker Book House, 1991.

Van Engen, Charles Edward, and Jude Tiersma. *God so Loves the City: Seeking a Theology for Urban Mission*. Monrovia, CA: MARC, 1994.

Van Engen, Charles Edward, Nancy J Thomas, and Robert L Gallagher. *Footprints of God: A Narrative Theology of Mission*. Monrovia, CA: MARC, 1999.

Vang, Preben. *Telling God's Story: The Biblical Narrative from Beginning to End*. Nashville: Broadman & Holman Publishers, 2006.

Veltman, Calvin. *Language Shift in the United States*. Berlin: Mouton Press, 1983.

Venn, Henry. "On Steps Towards Helping a Native Church to Become Self-Supporting, Self-Governing and Self-Extending." In *To Apply the Gospel: Selections from the Writings of Henry Venn*, ed. Max Warren. Grand Rapids: William B. Eerdmans Publishing Company, 1971.

Wacquant, L. "The New Urban Color Line: The State and Fate of the Ghetto in Post-Fordist America." In *Social theory and the Politics of Identity*, ed. C. Calhoun. Oxford: Blackwell, 1994.

Wagner, C. Peter. *Church Planting for a Greater Harvest: A Comprehensive Guide.* Ventura, CA: Regal Books, 1990.

Wan, Enoch, ed. *Diaspora Missiology: Theory, Methodology, and Practice.* Portland, OR: Institute of Diaspora Studies – U.S., 2011.

Warner, W. Lloyd, and Leo Srole. *The Social Systems of American Ethnic Groups.* New Haven, CT: Yale University Press, 1945.

Watters, Ethan. *Urban Tribes: Are Friends the New Family?* London: Bloomsbury Publishing PLC, 2004.

Whiteman, Darrell. "Anthropological Reflections on Contextualizing Theology in a Globalizing World." In *Globalizing Theology: Belief and Practice in an Era of World Christianity*, ed. Craig Ott and Harold Netland. Grand Rapids: Baker Academic, 2006.

Whiteman, M. Farr. *Writing: The Nature, Development, and Teaching of Written Communication.* Hillside, NH: Lawrence Erlbaum Associates, 1981.

Willis, Avery T., and Mark Snowden. *Truth that Sticks: How to Communicate Velcro Truth in a Teflon World.* Colorado Springs, CO: NavPress, 2010.

Willis, Avery, and Steve Evans. *Making Disciples of Oral Learners.* Lima, NY: International Orality Network, 2007.

Winter, Ralph D. and Steven C. Hawthorne. *Perspectives on the World Christian Movement: A Reader.* Rev. Ed. Pasadena, CA: William Carey Library, 1992.

Woodberry, John Dudley. *Muslims and Christians on the Emmaus road.* Monrovia, CA: MARC Publications, 1989.

Wright, John W. *Telling God's Story: Narrative Preaching for Christian Formation.* Downers Grove, IL: IVP Academic, 2007.

York, Herschael, and Bart Decker. *Preaching with Bold Assurance: A Solid and Enduring Approach to Engaging Exposition.* Nashville: Broadman and Holman Publishers, 2003.

Young, M., and P. Willmott. *Family and Kinship in East London.* Middlesex, U.K.: Penguin, 1957.

Zhou, Min. *Chinatown: The Socioeconomic Potential of an Urban Enclave.* Philadelphia: Temple University Press, 1992.

Articles

Archer, Kenneth. "A Pentecostal Way of Doing Theology: Method and Manner."
    International Journal of Systematic Theology 9 (2007): 306.

Badgero, Ray, and Harvie Conn. "Visual Aids for Missions Instructors."
    Evangelical Missions Quarterly 21 (1985): 413-15.

Bailey, Kenneth. "Informal Controlled Oral Tradition and the Synoptic Gospels." *Asia Journal of Theology* 5 (1991): 34-54.

Bailey, Thomas, and Roger Waldinger. "Primary, Secondary and Enclave Labor Markets: A Training System Approach." *American Sociological Review* 56 (1991): 432-45.

Boaz, Franz. "The Folklore of the Eskimo." *Journal of American Folklore* 64 (1904): 2.

Boomershine, Thomas E. "Jesus of Nazareth and the Watershed of Ancient Orality and Literacy." *Semeia* 65 (1994): 7-36.

Bush, Troy. "Urbanizing Panta ta Ethne." *The Journal of Evangelism and Missions* 12 (Spring 2013): 3-16.

Buswell, James Oliver. "Conn on Functionalism and Presupposition in Missionary Anthropology." *Trinity Journal* 7, no. 2 (1986): 69-95.

Camery-Hoggatt, Jerry. "The Word of God from Living Voices: Orality and Literacy in the Pentecostal Tradition." *PNEUMA* 27 (2005): 249.

Clarke, Clifton R. "Old Wine and New Wine Skins: West Indian and the New West African Pentecostal Churches in Britain and the Challenge of Renewal." *Journal of Pentecostal Theology* 19 (2010): 143–54.

Conn, Harvie M. "Counseling in Urban Missions." *Urban Mission* 9 (1991): 3-58.

_____. "Research in Urban Ministry for Church Growth and Planting." *Urban Mission* 8 (1991): 3-64.

_____. "Spiritual Warfare and Urban Missions." *Urban Mission* 13 (1995): 3-63.

_____. "Contextual Theologies: The Problem of Agendas." *Westminster Theological Journal* 52 (1990): 51-63.

_____. "Evangelizing the Urban Centers of the World." *Review & Expositor* 90 (1993): 67-81.

_____. "God's Urban Surprises." *Urban Mission* 14 (1997): 3-6.

_____. "Looking at Some of Africa's Urban Challenges." *Urban Mission* 16 (1998): 3-6.

_____. "Looking to the Future: Evangelical Missions from North America in the Years Ahead." *Urban Mission* 5 (1988): 18-31.

_____. "Lucan Perspectives and the City." *Missiology* 13 (1985): 409-428.

_____. "Refugees, the City, and Missions." *Urban Mission* 15 (1997): 3-6.

_____. "Spiritual Warfare in the City." *Urban Mission* 13 (1995): 3-8.

_____. "The City, Violence, and Jesus." *Urban Mission* 11 (1994): 3-5.

_____. "The City: The New Frontier." *Evangelical Missions Quarterly* 20 (1984): 395-398.

_____. "The Invisible Minority." *Urban Mission* 10 (1993): 3-5.

_____. "The Rural-Urban Myth and World Mission." *Reformed Review* 37 (1984): 125-136.

_____. "The Urban Elite." *Urban Mission* 13 (1996): 3-6.

_____. "Theological Education for the City." *Urban Mission* 10 (1992): 3-5.

_____. "Urban Mission : Where Are We Now?" *Urban Mission* 16 (1999): 3-5.

Davis, Casey Wayne. "Hebrews 6:4-6 from an Oral Critical Perspective." *Journal of the Evangelical Theological Society* 51 (2008): 754.

Dewey, Joanna. "From Storytelling to Written Text : The Loss of Early Christian Women's Voices." *Biblical Theology Bulletin* 26 (1996): 71-78.

_____. "Oral Methods of Structuring Narrative in Mark." *Interpretation* 43 (1989): 32-44.

_____. "Textuality in an Oral Culture : A Survey of the Pauline Traditions." *Semeia*, 65 (1994): 37-65.

Foster, Stuart. "Oral Theology in Lomwe Songs." *International Bulletin of Missionary Research* 32 (2008): 130.

Gee, James. "Orality and Literacy: From *The Savage Mind* to *Ways with Words*." *TESOL Quarterly* 20 (1986): 719-46.

Gilbertson, Greta. "Women's Labor and Enclave Employment: The Case of Dominican and Colombian Women in New York City." *International Migration Review* 29 (1993):657-70.

Gilbertson, Greta and Douglas Gurak. "Broadening the Enclave Debate: The Labor Market Experiences of Dominican and Colombian Men in New York City." *Sociological Forum* 8 (1993): 205-20.

Goody, Jack. "The Consequences of Literacy." *Comparative Studies in History and Society* 5 (1963): 304-45.

Greenway, Roger S. "The 'Team' Approach to Urban Church Planting." *Urban Mission* 4 (1987): 3-5.

Hiebert, Paul G. "Planting Churches in North America Today." *Direction* 20 (Fall 1991): 6-14.

Hill, Harriet. "Conversations about Orality." *Missiology* 38 (April 2010): 215-17.

Houghton, Graham, and Ezra Sargunam. "The Role of Theological Education in Church Planting Among the Urban Poor: A Case Study from Madras." *Evangelical Review of Theology* 6 (1982): 141-44.

Ito, Akio. "The Written Torah and the Oral Gospel: Romans 10:5-13 in the Dynamic Tension between Orality and Literacy," *Novum Testamentum* 48 (2006), 245-46.

Jacobs, Jane. "The City Unbound: Qualitative Approaches to the City." *Urban Studies* (30): 827-48.

King, Roberta R. "Telling God's Story through Song." *Evangelical Missions Quarterly* 38 (2002): 295-96.

Klem, Herbert. "Bible as Oral Literature in Oral Societies." *International Review of Mission* 67 (1978): 479.

————. "Dependence on Literacy Strategy: Taking a Hard Second Look." *International Journal of Frontier Missions* 12:2 (1995): 63-64.

Kolb, Robert. "Urban Missions." *Missio apostolica* 7 (1999): 2-66.

Lenters, Kimberly. "No Half Measures: Reading Instruction for Young Second-language Learners." *Reading Teacher* 58 (2004): 328–36.

Lovejoy, Grant. "The Extent of Orality: 2012 Update." *Orality Journal: The Word became Fresh* 1 (2012): 12.

Mar, Don. "Another Look at the Enclave Economy Thesis: Chinese Immigrants in the Ethnic Labor Market." *Amerasia Journal* 17 (1991): 5-21.

Martin, Bruce. "Urban Ministry in Canada." *Urban Mission* 15 (1997): 3-63.

Mbiti, John S. "Cattle are Born with Ears, their Horns Grow Later: Towards an Appreciation Of African Oral Theology." In *All African Lutheran Consultation on Christian Theology and Christian Education for the African Context.* Geneva: LWF, 1978, 50.

McLean, Janice. "Make a Joyful Noise Unto the Lord: Music and Songs Within Pentecostal West Indian Immigrant Religious Communities in Diaspora." *Studies in World Christianity* 13 (2007): 127–41.

Naude, Piet. "Theology with a New Voice? The Case for an Oral Theology in the South African Context." *Journal of Theology for Southern Africa* 94 (1996): 22.

Nee, Victor, Jimy Sanders, and Scott Sernau. "Job Transitions in an Immigrant Metropolis: Ethnic Boundaries and the Mixed Economy." *American Sociological Review* 59 (December 1994): 849-72.

Ortiz, Manuel. "An Urgent Call to Do Mission in Our Cities : A Missiological Challenge." *Evangelical Journal* 16 (1998): 1-12.

_____. "Circle Church: A Case Study in Contextualization." *Urban Mission* 8 (1991): 6-18.

_____. "My Commitment to Intercultural Christian Community: An Hispanic Pilgrimage." *Urban Mission* 12 (1994): 14-24.

_____. "The Church and the City." *Themelios* 28 (2003): 49-63.

_____. "The Multiethnic Church in the US." *Urban Mission* 13 (1996): 3-58.

Paul, Dierdre Glenn. "Rap and Orality: Critical Media Literacy, Pedagogy, and Cultural Synchronization." *Journal of Adolescent & Adult Literacy* 44 (2000): 246.

Ponraj, S Devasahayam, and Chandon K. Sah. "Communication Bridges to Oral Cultures: A Method that Caused a Breakthrough in Starting Several Church Planting Movements in North India." *International Journal of Frontier Missions* 20 (2003): 28-31.

Prior, Randall. "Orality: The Not-So-Silent Issue in Mission Theology." *International Bulletin for Missionary Research* (2011): 145.

Ray, Chandu. "The Use of Dance-Drama in Evangelism." *Effective Evangelism* 1 (1971): 8.

Rynkiewich, Michael. "Mission, Hermeneutics, and the Local Church." *Journal of Theological Interpretation* 1 (2007): 50-51.

Sawatsky, Ben A. "A Church Planting Strategy for World Class Cities." *Urban Mission* 3 (1985): 7-19.

Schuegraf, Oliver. "Telling God's Stories Again and Again: Reflection on Remembrance and Reconciliation." *Modern Believing* 47 (2006): 31-42.

Shelley, Mark. "Planting Ethnic Churches: An Urban Priority." *Urban Mission* 12 (1995): 7-15.

Snowden, Mark. "Tools for Listening: Quantitative and Qualitative." *Evangelical Missions Quarterly* 41 (2005): 496-503.

Steffen, Tom. "A Narrative Approach to Communicating the Bible." *Christian Education Journal* 14 (1994): 86-97.

_____. "Developing and Disseminating a Life-Changing Curriculum." *Evangelical Review of Theology* 20 (1996): 273-82.

_____. "Don't Show the 'Jesus' Film . . : To Maximize the Potential of this Powerful Evangelistic Tool, We Need to do our Homework First." *Evangelical Missions Quarterly* 29 (1993): 272-75.

_____. "Flawed Evangelism and Church Planting: When our Methods are Flawed, Does the Holy Spirit Step in as Clean-Up Hitter?" *Evangelical Missions Quarterly* 34 (1998): 428-35.

_____. "Foundational Roles of Symbol and Narrative in the (Re)construction of Reality and Relationships." *Missiology* 26 (1998): 477-94.

_____. "How User-Friendly is your Teaching." *Evangelical Missions Quarterly* 32 (1996): 178-85.

_____. "My Journey from Propositional to Narrative Evangelism." *Evangelical Missions Quarterly* 41 (2005): 200-06.

_____. "Pedagogical Conversions: From Propositions to Story and Symbol." *Missiology* 38 (2010): 141-59.

_____. "Producing Quality Training Through Partnerships: Assemblies, Academics, and Agencies." *Journal of the American Society for Church Growth* 8 (Winter 1997): 53-61.

_____. "Reaching 'Resistant' People through Intentional Narrative." *Missiology* 28 (2000): 471-86.

_____. "Selecting a Church Planting Model That Works." *Missiology* 22 (1994): 361-76.

_____. "Storying the Storybook to Tribals: A Philippines Perspective of the Chronological Teaching Model." *International Journal of Frontier Missions* 12 (1995): 99-104.

_____. "Training Institutions Ignore the Basics--Or Do They: Second Response." *International Journal of Frontier Missions* 11 (1994): 53-55.

_____. "Urban-Rural Networks and Strategies." *Urban Mission* 10 (1993): 37-42.

Steffen, Tom, and James O. Terry. "The Sweeping Story of Scripture Taught through Time." *Missiology* 35 (2007): 315-35.

Strauss, Robert, and Tom Steffen. "Change the Worldview...Change the World." *Evangelical Missions Quarterly* 45 (2009): 458-64.

Street, Brian. "New Literacies in Theory and Practice: What are the Implications for Language in Education?" *Linguistics and Education 10* (1998): 1-24.

Stutterheim, Ernst. "Wildflowers in the Desert: The Joys and Trials of Urban Church Planting." *Urban Mission* 15 (1997): 26-35.

Terry, J.O. "The Worldwide Spread of Bible Storying: A Look at Where We've Been." *Orality Journal: The Word Became Fresh* 1 (2012): 41-62.

Thomas, Günter. "Secondary Ritualization in a Postliterate Culture: Reconsidering and Expanding Walter Ong's Contribution on 'Secondary Orality'." *Soundings* 83 (2000): 385-409.

Tino, James, and Paul Brink. "A Model for Urban Church Planting The First Phase: From Preliminary Investigation to First Worship Service." *Missio apostolica* 7 (1999): 40-46.

Westgate, James E. "Emerging Church Planting Strategies for World Class Cities." *Urban Mission* 4 (1986): 6-13.

Williams, Brett. "Poverty Among African Americans in the Urban United States." *Human Organization* 51 (1992): 164-73.

Zelinsky, Wilbur and Barrett Lee. "Heterolocalism: An Alternative Model of the Sociospatial Behaviour of Immigrant Ethnic Communities." *International Journal of Population Geography* 4 (1998): 281.

Dissertations

Barnes, Philip. "Missiology Meets Cultural Anthropology: The Life and Legacy of Paul G. Hiebert." PhD diss., Southern Baptist Theological Seminary, 2011.

Daniel, Angelane. "Ong's Great Leap: The Politics of Literacy and Orality." PhD Diss., University of Texas at Austin, 1986.

Johnson, Wendal Mark. "Mentoring Program for Urban Missionary Apprentices of the International Mission Board Serving in Brazil." DMiss diss., The Southern Baptist Theological Seminary, 2012.

Kuenzel, Bruce A. "Can you Tell me how to Get to Sesame Street": The Recovery of the Orality of Preaching in an Electronic Age." DMin diss., Lutheran School of Theology at Chicago, 2001.

Lee, Kuem Ju. "Bible Storying: A Recommended Strategy for Training Church Leaders in Oral Societies." PhD diss., The Southern Baptist Theological Seminary, 2005.

Lin, Meixiao. "Effects of Cooperative Learning on the Oral Proficiency of Chinese Students in the Teritary-Level EFL Classroom." PhD diss., University of Leicester, 2011.

Miller, Lorraine Jennifer. "The Transition from Orality to Literacy in the Anglo-Saxon Kingdoms." PhD diss., University of Wales, College of Cardiff, 1990.

Walters, Jeffrey K. "'Effective Evangelism' in the City: Donald McGavran's Missiology and Urban Contexts." PhD diss., The Southern Baptist Theological Seminary, 2011.

Online

Abney, Lynne. "Orality Assessment Tool Worksheet." www.orality.net/sites/default/ files/Orality_ Assessment_Tool_Worksheet.pdf (accessed September 4, 2013).

Casey, Anthony. "A Missiological Portrait of Bombay, India." Unpublished paper, 2010. http://culturnicity.files.wordpress.com/2011/04/bombayfinal.pdf (accessed September 3, 2013).

_____. "Making It in the United States: A Study of Nepali Refugees at an Apartment Complex in Louisville, KY." http://culturnitiy.files.wordpress.com /2011/04/nepali-ethnography1.pdf (accessed September 4, 2013).

Casey, Anthony, ed. "London Ethnography." http://culturnicity.files.wordpress.com /2011/04/london-ethnography.pdf (accessed September 4, 2013).

City of Louisville. "Office for Globalization." http://www.louisvilleky.gov/Globalization/ (accessed September 4, 2013).

Cru Press. "The Compass." http://crupressgreen.com/compass/ (accessed September 4, 2013).

Eknazar Desi Lifestyle Portal. http://eknazar.com (accessed September 3, 2013).

International Mission Board. "Orality Strategies." http://www.oralitystrategies.org (accessed September 4, 2013).

Kentucky Refugee Ministries. http://kyrm.org/ (accessed September 4, 2013).

Lausanne Occasional Paper 54. "Making Disciples of Oral Learners." Edited by David Claydon. http://www.lausanne.org/en/documents/lops/870-lop-54.html (accessed July 26, 2013).

Mizrach, Steven. "From Orality to Teleliteracy." http://www.fiu.edu/~mizrachs/ orality.htm (accessed September 4, 2012).

Moon, Lottie. "Correspondence with Henry A. Tupper on 17 July 1885." http://solomon .3e2a.org/public/ws/lmcorr/www2/lmcorrp /Record? upp=0&m=20&w= NATIVE%28%27text+ph+is+%27%27preaching %27%27%27%29& r=1&order=native% 28%27corr_date%2FDescend%27%29 (accessed November 18, 2010).

————. "Correspondence with Henry A. Tupper on 10 October 1878." http:// solomon.3e2a.org/public/ws/lmcorr/www2/lmcorrp/Record?upp=0&m=2 2&w=NATIVE%28%27text+ph+is+%27%27preaching%27%27%27%29&r= 1&order=native%28%27corr_date%2FDescend%27%29 (accessed November 18, 2010).

North American Mission Board and International Mission Board. "People Groups Info." http://www.peoplegroups.info/ (accessed September 4, 2013).

Office of Refugee Resettlement. "State Profiles." http://www.acf.hhs.gov/programs/orr/ data/state_profiles.htm (accessed September 4, 2013).

Pandya, Chhandasi. "Limited English Proficient Workers and the Workforce Investment Act: Challenges and Opportunities." http://www.migrationinformation.org/Feature /display.cfm?ID=900 (accessed August 29, 2012).

Refuge Ministries. http://refugelouisville.com (accessed September 4, 2013).

Sills, David. "Missiology in a Changing World Since WWII." http://www.asmweb.org/ content/ previous-meetings (accessed September 3, 2013).

U.S. Bureau of the Census. "Growth in Urban Population Outpaces Rest of Nation." http:// www.census.gov/newsroom/releases/archives/2010_census/cb12-50.html (accessed September 3, 2013).

Made in the USA
Columbia, SC
07 November 2017